DEVELOPING AND DELIVERING YOUR MESSAGE

A Guide to Public Speaking

Cameron Basquiat

Dr. Jennifer Huss Basquiat

Dr. Timothy James

HOUGHTON MIFFLIN COMPANY
Boston   New York

Custom Publishing Editor: Peter Nowka
Custom Publishing Production Manager: Kathleen McCourt
Custom Publishing Project Coordinator: Christina Battista

Cover Designer: Faith Duldulao

Acknowledgements: page 44: reproduced by permission of Google Inc., page 28: photograph of women, http://mathworld.wolfram.com/YoungGirl-OldWomanIllusion.html.

Printed in the United States of America.

ISBN: 0-618-50594-6
N-03448

1 2 3 4 5 6 7 8 9 – CCI – 06 05 04

222 Berkeley Street • Boston, MA 02116

Address all correspondence and order information to the above address.

Course Information

Your Name _____

Course Section Number _____

Meeting Days/Times _____

Classroom _____

Instructor's name _____

Instructor's Contact Information (phone number/ office number/ E-mail)

_____

_____

_____

_____

_____

Preface

Objectives

Welcome to COM 101: Oral Communication at CCSN. While you may have signed up for this class to meet a particular graduation requirement this class may turn out to be one of the most valuable courses you will take. In this class you will develop skills to become a more effective communicator. In particular you will learn how to perform research, construct a well-organized speech, incorporate evidence and reasoning to support your ideas and ultimately deliver your message to an audience.

The skills you will develop will serve you well in the remainder of your academic career and well beyond. The ability to clearly express your ideas, whether though oral or written communication, allows you to convey messages that are important you. The skill of effective communication is highly sought after in a variety of professional fields including education, business, government and law.

This book is designed to help you best develop your skills. In this book you will find exercises designed to help you reduce your communication anxiety, brainstorm for speech topics, research information, organize your thoughts and support them with strong evidence and deliver your speech with more confidence.

Remember, this book is designed to help you understand the fundamentals of public speaking and to serve as a tool to help you develop your oral communication skills. In cases of conflict with what you learn in your class, always defer to what your instructor requires for each of your assignments.

Acknowledgements

We would like to thank several individuals who contributed to this textbook: Eric Moreau for his ideas and assistance with the chapter on Communication Anxiety; Loretta Fearonce for her assistance in the construction on the section focusing on Plagiarism (in the chapter on Research); Belle Tumbucon and Kristin Marshall, two outstanding students who contributed their original speech outlines (with minor modifications). We also want to thank our colleagues at the Community College of Southern Nevada for both supporting and using this textbook. They make our department a place that is both inviting and comfortable to be. Also, it is important to acknowledge the valuable input and editorial assistance we received from the best custom publishing editor in the business: Peter Nowka.

Cameron Basquiat
Jennifer Huss Basquiat, Ph.D.
Timothy James, Ph.D.

Tips for Success in this Course

1) **Attendance:** Each day in class is important. Some days you will learn from your instructor's lectures or prepared assignments. Other days you will be watching your fellow students giving their speeches. And yes, some days you will be the one speaking. Each of these occasions offers multiple learning opportunities. The more you are in class the better you will do in the course.

2) **Attitude:** Though the prospect of public speaking may be intimidating, remember that you are in this class to develop a necessary skill. Also, your fear is not uncommon. According to Steven A. Beebe, author of *Public Speaking*, "in a survey seeking to identify people's phobias, public speaking ranked as the most anxiety-producing experience most people face."[1] Your instructor and fellow students are all in this together with one goal: Improving your ability and skills. Remember: YOU CAN SUCCEED!

3) **Complete all assigned readings:** This textbook, lecture notes, and handouts all offer valuable information designed to improve your oral communication abilities.

4) **Class participation:** Be active in class discussion. Ask questions. Share ideas. All of these will deepen your understanding of the assignments in the class.

5) **Invest time on Speech development:** The steps of coming up with the right topic, narrowing that topic into the best speech, researching and organizing your information and then writing the speech is a lengthy process. Start working on your speeches well in advance of the due date.

6) **Practice your speeches:** After writing your speech make sure you practice it over and over. The more you practice it out loud (preferably to an audience) the more accustomed you will become with the speech. In turn, your anxiety will decrease as your familiarity with the speech increases.

7) **Review feedback:** After you have given your speech you will receive feedback from the instructor and/or from your fellow students. Examine the feedback for comments that can help you improve your next presentation. Use each assignment as a stepping-stone to becoming a better speaker.

---

[1] Beebe, S., & Beebe, S. (2000). *Public Speaking: An Audience-Centered Approach.* (4th Edition). Boston: Allyn and Bacon, 18.

Table of Contents

1 *Being a Communicator*

Terms to Know

- Communication
- Negotiation of Meaning
- Transactional Model of Communication
- Sender (Speaker)
- Sender intent
- Receiver (Audience)
- Receiver intent
- Encoding
- Symbol system
- Channel
- Feedback (Response)
- Noise
- Communication setting

Communication is one of the most fundamental processes in which we engage daily. From the moment we awake and begin to talk to ourselves, we engage in symbolic activities that give us a sense of who we are, what we're doing, why we're doing it, how to do it, etc.

But communication isn't a mere matter of just talking. When you have a conversation with a friend, for example, far more is going on than just a mere exchange of words. You have to assess the nature of the interaction (is this serious? is this joking? is there a specific outcome either of you desire?); you have to assess the nature of the messages that you both create and interpret (what DO you mean by "I love you?"); you have to assess the other person's body language and gestures; and you have to assess the setting in which you are conversing (what are you allowed to say or not say in this instance?).

Indeed, the more you examine any one instance of communication between two or more people, the more you begin to see that **communication is an ongoing, changing, and dynamic process that requires all parties involved to be aware of many elements that make communication more or less effective.**

Consider, for instance, just a few of the elements that can go into a public presentation:

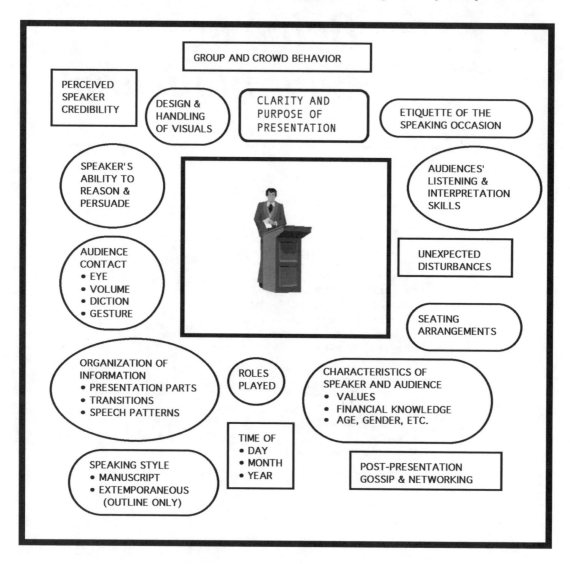

Most people who are suddenly assigned to give a presentation probably don't think about all of these matters. Like most of your fellow classmates, you're probably thinking in terms of "oh, jeez, I have to get up there in front of a bunch of people and give a speech!" (Fear not. Ways to deal with your anxieties are covered in another chapter!)

You probably don't give much, if any, thought to all of these other elements. If you want to have a truly effective and successful presentation experience, however, you need to learn what's involved in communication and how to gain control over those aspects of the communication process that are within your ability to manage. In many cases, you already do this in your daily life, even though you may not be consciously aware of it.

This chapter will give you some idea of how you can better take control of your speaking situations. At the least, it will help you begin to see that you have certain responsibilities to attend to as a communicator.

Types of Communication

There are many ways to look at and understand the nature of communication. One way is to examine the many different kinds of communication in which we can engage. Let's consider just a simple layout of the instances in which communication occurs:

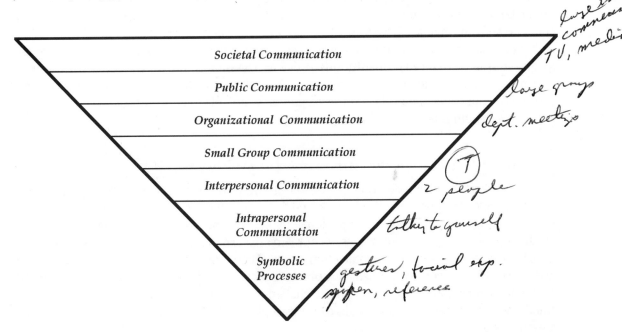

Here, we see that at a most basic level, we have to engage in symbolic processes. These can consist of different types of spoken and written languages, gestures, facial expressions, body language, etc. In the simplest of terms, if you want to communicate with someone, you have to use symbols and follow common rules for using those symbols (e.g., the rules of grammar).

At an intrapersonal communication level, you are involved in self-talk. We all talk to ourselves, and even though some people may think this is crazy, the fact is that we would not be able to function if we didn't engage in self-dialog. Even during a presentation, you are probably wondering to yourself whether you're being clear, whether your audience is responding as you would like, how well you're doing on your speech, and so on.

Interpersonal communication takes place between two people. This can take place in any configuration, from two strangers who meet on the street to intimate relations between people who have known each other for years. Different communication roles also begin to emerge here, such as supervisor and employee, professor and student, or speaker and audience.

When we begin to add a few more people, we begin to see communication take place in small groups. Groups have their own sense of dynamics, and the rules for how to interact are often considerably different than between just two people. Indeed, speaking in small groups is a form of public presentation, since you often have several people attending to what you have to say.

At an organizational level—such as communication between departments at CCSN—we begin to see that interaction becomes more challenging to manage. People often know and encounter one another less formally, and communication often becomes less personal than it would at the interpersonal or small group level. It also becomes increasingly possible for the intended meanings of our messages to be misconstrued, garbled, etc. since we have less opportunity to clarify our messages. (If you're face-to-face, you can immediately ask questions of the other person to clarify what they said.)

Public communication can take several forms, such as giving a presentation to a large group of people. As with organizational communication, we often encounter the problem of trying to deliver messages to relative strangers. Our communication can, again, seem to be less personal, and we may have less control over how others interpret and act on the messages we intend to convey. As you'll learn in the chapter on delivery, however, one of the primary goals of good public speaking is to try to overcome some of this impersonal nature of public communication. With practice, you can develop a rather personal-sounding style that can enhance an audiences' understanding of you and that can help minimize some of the potential misunderstandings that could arise from what you have to say.

Societal communication here refers to communication by large institutions, such as the media. Messages produced by institutions—such as television commercials—often are the products of a number of individuals and agencies. As such, at this level, communication becomes extremely impersonal, and it becomes exceptionally difficult to control the kinds of meanings and understandings people produce for messages.

How Communication Works—A Transactional Model

The preceding discussion on types of communication suggests a few themes that are central to an understanding of public speaking and the communication process in general: messages, their meaning(s), and the level(s) of personal involvement people have in the overall process of producing and interpreting messages. As our personal experiences in communicating probably have taught us over the years, it would often be nice if communication could be as simple as "here are my words" and everyone immediately understands them and responds as we hope they would. Alas, communication is often much more challenging and imprecise than that; but an understanding of how communication works can at least give us a better idea of how to gain some measure of control over the process.

One of the most basic ways of understanding communication is to look at is as a transaction, wherein two or more parties negotiate the meanings of each others' words, often with a common goal that both want to achieve. Please do not confuse this view of communication as a mere exchange of words. The emphasis here is on the **negotiation of meaning**, not a simple exchange of meanings.

To negotiate meaning implies that our words often can mean more than one thing, and all parties involved in any given instance of communication need to make efforts to (1) try to choose words carefully and (2) try to understand words carefully. (See, also, the chapter on listening in this book!) How does this process work?

Well, there are several key elements present in any communication, regardless of what type of communication we're considering. The model on the next page shows the relationships among these elements, and a discussion of each will follow.

This view of the **transactional model** of communication is obviously taking place in an interpersonal type of communication. This is more familiar to most of us, so it's a good place to begin examining the nature of communication. In a moment, we'll explore it in a public speaking setting. For now, however, let's focus on the key elements of this model.

The **sender** is the person who is speaking at any given moment. It is assumed that the sender has some kind of **intent** in communicating; he or she wants to achieve some kind of outcome. Intent could be something as simple as continuing a conversation or perhaps it could involve a desire to get the other person to take some specific action.

In order to make this intent known to someone else, the sender has to encode a message. **Encoding** involves the use of one or more symbol systems, such as language. A **symbol system** involves words, gestures, images, etc. that follow some set of rules. For instance, if you wish to speak in English, you have to choose words within that vocabulary and follow rules for how to construct a sensible sentence. If you wish to construct a television commercial (at the

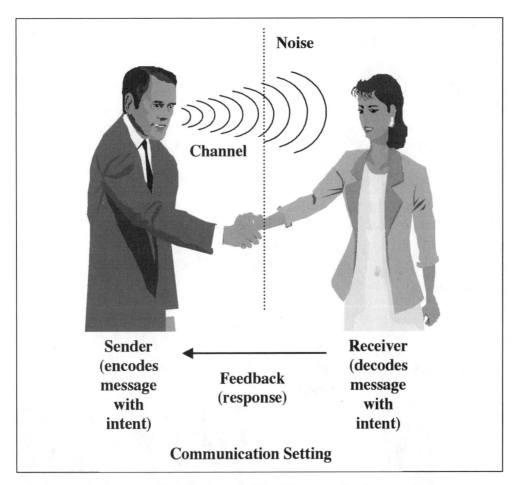

A Transaction Model of Communication

societal level of communication), you would also have to choose various kinds of camera shots, follow certain rules of editing, etc.

The choice of which symbol system(s) to use often goes hand in hand with the channel by which the message will be sent. The **channel** is the means by which the message is transmitted. For instance, the speaker in our model is choosing a verbal means of communication (i.e., he's talking). But he could also put the same message in a written note, call the other person on the phone, or via videoconference.

The person who receives the message is the receiver. If the receiver wishes to participate in communication with the sender, then he or she will have to put in some effort. (Here again, see the chapter on listening for more information.) Upon hearing the sender's message, he or she will have to decode it. **Decoding** means making sense of a sender's message and involved determining what the symbols are supposed to mean.

Note that the receiver also decodes messages with **intent**, just as the sender has a certain intent. That intent may or may not be the same as the sender's; for instance, perhaps the receiver wants to change the topic of conversation.

Regardless of the receiver's particular intent, he or she will have some kind of **response** to the sender's message and provide **feedback** by sending a message of his or her own. At this point, the receiver has now become the sender, and the communication roles are reversed.

In the midst of this process are two factors that contribute to the nature of the interaction. First, there are various kinds of **noise** which can interfere with the intentions of the communicators. Such noise can be physical, such as when it's hard to hear someone speak at a noisy concert. Noise could also be semantic, wherein there is a lack of clarity about what words or other symbols mean. If someone says "I love you," it could mean "as a friend," or "romantically," or perhaps even jokingly.

Second, all communication takes place in some kind of **setting**, or context. The communication setting could best be defined as the roles and rules we are expected to follow in order to behave appropriately. We always look to the setting to help us make sense of how to proceed in our communications. For instance, you could have a conversation about a movie you just saw. The nature of your conversation is likely to be very different if it's among friends at a restaurant than if it's in a classroom discussion. With your friends, you can be more relaxed and feel free to say things that you might not want to share in the middle of a class.

Putting it Into Practice: Your Role as a Speaker

Now that we've seen the elements of communication in an interpersonal setting, let's look at how these elements work in public speaking. Let's look at the transactional model again, only this time, we'll substitute some of the images and labels:

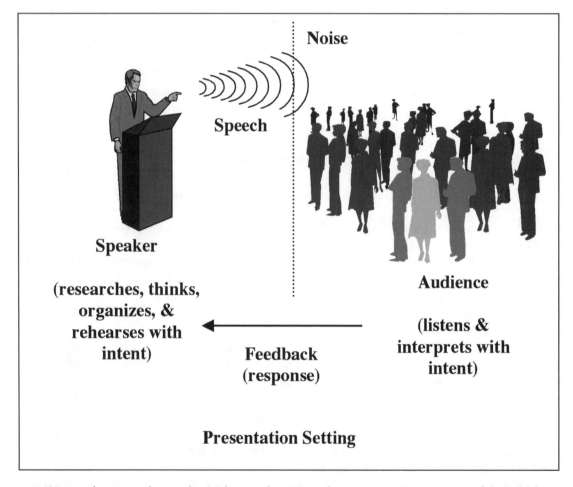

Here, of course, the sender is the speaker. Note that among many aspects of the speaker's intent, there are four key ingredients: research, thought, organization, and rehearsal. These ingredients are covered in detail throughout this book. For now, you can at least realize that the speaker has several responsibilities in order to help make a presentation effective. These are discussed in the next section of this chapter.

All of these speaker efforts eventually materialize as the actual speech. Note that the speech itself—the words, gestures, and presentation aids that you deliver—is only one of several elements of the presentation setting. The speech itself is only the channel by which the speaker's intent is made available to the audience. Focusing only on the things you say—without also focusing on the other elements of the presentation—is not what "giving a speech" is all about. You have to look at the whole picture and prepare for it.

Audience members are, of course, the receivers. They listen to, interpret, and respond to all of these elements as well. They do not focus only on "the speech," although a good deal of their attention is (hopefully) focused there. As a member of this class, you want to learn to become an effective audience member, not just a speaker.

Effective speakers take all aspects of the setting into account when preparing for and giving a presentation. No two speaking situations are alike, and you have to learn to adapt to a variety of changing circumstances.

As the previous model indicated, if you are going to give a presentation, you are obligated to the four characteristics of speaker intent: research, thought, organization, and rehearsal. In addition, you also need to recognize your role in the overall presentation setting. Here, it's important to develop a good attitude from the very beginning, starting with a transactional model of public speaking.

The transactional model should help you better see how an effective speaker should think. Inexperienced or ineffective speakers will tend to focus too much on the "speech" and not enough on other factors that are involved in presentations. For instance, they may focus on what gets written and said without actually considering the more fundamental question of "to whom am I speaking?"

This "speech-centered" model makes presentations sound like a one-way process.

From this point of view, all you have to do is write the speech, deliver the words, and you're done. The audience gets treated as sort of a by-product, or maybe even a nuisance or a threat. For instance, in an episode of the Brady Bunch, Marsha has to give a speech, and her father gives her advice on how to deal with her fear: picture your audience in their underwear. One might ask, however, why a speaker needs to begin with an attitude that the audience is an enemy whose power must be removed.

In the transactional model, however, you have to be more strategic and involved. The writing and delivery of the speech is not a one-way process. Both you and the audience will be involved in what your words, gestures, etc. all mean. You might not be able to control every aspect of how they'll interpret and respond to you, but you will at least have facilitated a set of conditions that can increase your likelihood for a successful experience.

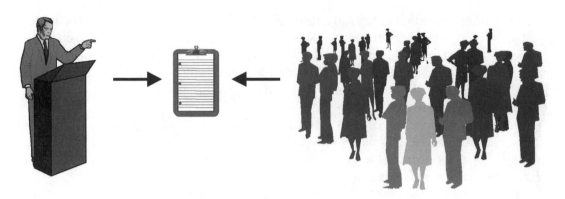

A transactional model recognizes that all parties play a role in the meanings of your words

EXERCISES

1) In small groups, discuss what happens if you remove any of the elements of the transactional process. For example, what would happen if you could remove all forms of noise? How realistic is this?

2) In small groups, pretend you are a consulting group to whom a speaker has come for advice. Invent a speech topic and a particular type of presentation setting (e.g., giving a speech about the Civil War to your history class). Then describe the characteristics of the audience; be specific. Continue to describe all of the different elements. Be creative; for example, you could create a scenario where the speaker doesn't have a podium. After you've described all of the elements, explain to the speaker how he or she should best proceed in this particular speaking situation.

2 *Communication Anxiety*

Terms to Know

- State Anxiety
- Physiological Indicators
- Psychological Indicators
- Negative Self-Talk
- Self-Pressuring
- Self-Criticizing
- Catastrophizing
- Cognitive Restructuring
- Self-Fulfilling Prophecy
- Coping Statements
- Visualization

What's scarier than giving a speech in public? Not much, if you asked the majority of Americans. You might be surprised to learn that recent studies suggest that 85 % of the population has some anxiety over public speaking and that 40% of Americans list Public speaking as their greatest fear? So if you have put off taking this course until your last semester, or changed you major in hopes that you wouldn't have to take this course you are not alone. But there is hope. In fact there is a variety of proven methods to help manage this communication anxiety. This chapter will go over nature of communication anxiety, how it is manifested in the body and brain, sources of anxiety and most importantly how to best manage the anxiety.

> I feel okay before the speech, but once my name is called to go and speak I feel a rush of panic. My palms get sweaty, and my heart races, I even struggle to keep my brain focused on my speech.
>
> --Rob, CCSN student

Communication anxiety involves the fear of giving an oral presentation in front of a live audience. This type of nervousness is categorized a type of **State Anxiety**, an uneasiness caused by a situation, like speaking in front of an audience. This fear is often accompanied by a variety of physical and emotional reactions that can greatly reduce a person's ability to successfully give a speech presentation.

The nervousness experienced can be groups into two categories of anxiety: Physiological indicators and Psychological indicators. **Physiological indicators** include all physical changes due to anxiety. These might include increased heart rate, perspiration, queasiness, dry mouth, and becoming flushed. **Psychological indicators** consist of any cognitive congestion including feeling like you cannot think clearly, or losing your train of thought. Other psychological indicators include anxiety not rooted in physiological changes, but in the *interpretation* of those changes. For example, noticing that your heart is racing and cognitively deciding that the increased heart rate means you won't give a good speech.

> In fourth grade I had to give an oral report on one of the United States. Half way through the speech I lost my place and couldn't get back on track. Some students started to laugh and then I really got scared. Ever since then I've been terrified of giving speeches.
>
> --Michelle, CCSN student

People get nervous before speaking for any number of legitimate reasons. To better understand some of the main reasons we feel nervousness we can explore six primary causes.

Sources of Anxiety

1) **Trauma**: Have you ever had an embarrassing moment when trying to give a speech? Sometimes a forgotten word, misquoted sentence, or other minor mistake can throw a speaker off his or her planned performance and lead to negative feelings about public speaking. When one has a negative experience sometimes those feelings linger and the event becomes a traumatic one that haunts the speaker whenever a presentation is in one's future.

2) **Speaking as performance**: Far too many people equate public speaking and acting. While the two activities both involve a public forum they are quite different in practice. Someone engaged in public speaking actively interacts with the audience, as indicated by the Transactional Model of Communication, the audience does communication with the speaker through nonverbal and verbal feedback. An actor typically does not interact with the audience. Public speaking often utilizes impromptu or extemporaneous speaking while most acting comes through memorization of a script. While a speech can be practiced it is no where as dependent on rehearsal and choreography as an actor is for a play. Typically a speaker is alone with his or her interaction with an audience whereas most acting involves multiple actors interacting with each other. Moreover, actors portray characters whereas speakers represent themselves. As you can see there are many differences between public speaking and acting. If you still disagree you need only watch most any acting award show to see the some of the "best" actors and actresses painfully stumble when giving a speech of acceptance for an award. Public speaking is a communication event whereas acting is a performance.

3) **Inexperience**: Often times it is our lack of experience with any activity that can cause anxiety to build. Imagine being asked to play the trombone in front of others with no practice, or having to throw a football for the first time. Most any new activity can inspire anxiety. You may not remember it but you parents may be able to tell some good tales about you struggles in learning to ride a bicycle. Fortunately, as with riding a bicycle, the anxiety you may feel with public speaking should reduce with practice and experience.

4) **Irrational Goals**: Despite the fact that most people do not have a substantial amount of experience in public speaking, far too many people think that they should inherently be successful at it. This false sense of confidence can lead to anxiety inducing beliefs that your speech should be flawless in all aspects.

5) **Lack of Preparedness**: Without considerable dedication to the research and organization of your speech as well as practicing your delivery you may find an overwhelming sense of anxiety when the time for that presentation arrives. As with most any challenging activity, commitment to being prepared for your speech is the first step to reducing your anxiety.

6) **Negative Self-talk**: Communication scholars Steve Brydon and Michael Scott define **negative self-talk** as an internal or intrapersonal communication act of self-defeating talk. There are three types of negative self-talk: self-pressuring, self-criticizing and catastrophizing.

   a. **Self-pressuring** is the act of self-talk in which a person puts an undue amount of pressure to succeed on oneself. For example, a statement like "I have to be perfect" indicates that excessive pressure.

   b. **Self-criticizing** involves the self-talk in which we berate ourselves. Dwelling on minor mistakes in your presentation or being overly critical of your speech would be some examples of self-criticizing behavior.

c. **Catastrophizing** involves blowing things out of proportion. Imagine hearing someone say, "I got poor grade on my speech and now I'll probably fail the class and never graduate and thus never get a good job."

It is important recognize the aforementioned sources of anxiety as the first step to managing your communication anxiety. But knowing the sources of anxiety is only the beginning. There seven specific steps you can follow toward managing your communication anxiety.

Managing Communication Anxiety

1) **Cognitive Restructuring**: The first step toward managing your anxiety is to change the way you think about the sensations you are experiencing. For example, Arousal and Anxiety both share the same physical symptoms, think about how your stress level changes if you consider sweaty palms or a racing heart as a sign of arousal instead of anxiety. Also, consider the popular source of anxiety of viewing public speaking as performance instead of communication. If you cognitively restructure giving a speech as an act of communication as an alternative to acting, does it change your anxiety level?

2) **Preparation and Practice**: While cognitive restructuring is the first step you must also do the tangible work. Completing your research, constructing your speech and then practicing your speech repeatedly will increase your confidence and conversely lower your communication anxiety.

3) **Setting Realistic Goals**: In addressing another source of anxiety, you can help reduce your unease by establishing reasonable goals. Instead of engaging self-pressing talk of trying to be perfect, set more reasonable targets like getting through the speech, improving on your last speech, or improving specific aspects of your delivery.

4) **Self-fulfilling prophecy**: The theory of **self-fulfilling prophecy** follows that if you feel strongly about either the success or failure of an event you can affect it in that direction. As such do not think about how you could fail, as this could increase the probability of disappointment with your presentation. Rather, using *positive* self-talk you increase the probability of success.

5) **Coping Statements**: One way to reduce your anxiety is to using **coping statements**. These statements are usually silent and internal and designed to ease your tension by focusing on the positive aspects of your presentation. Coping statement should occur prior to, during and after your presentation. Before your presentation remind yourself that you have done the necessary research and development of your speech, that you have practiced your presentation. During your speech focus on the positive, "I am doing well," "I know my speech," and "the audience seems to be interested in what I have to say." After your speech focus on the successes of your presentation. Review what you did correct in terms of organization and delivery.

6) **Relaxation Techniques**: There are number of physical activities that you can engage in prior to your presentation that should function to reduce your anxiety level. Exercise is a great, natural activity that can help you. Have you ever noticed how relaxed you feel a few hours after working out? Exercise stimulates the body and releases beta-blockers that inhibit aspects associated with increased anxiety. If possible engage in a mild workout two to four hours before you have to give a presentation. (Be sure you have time to get cleaned up before your speech.) If there is no time for working out there are activities you can do in most any location prior to giving your speech. Deep breathing, the tightening and relaxing muscles

through out your body, and safely rotating your head on your neck are all sample activities that may work as muscular relaxation.

7) **Visualization**: Drawing a mental picture, or visualization, of a successful presentation can help minimize your anxiety level. Used frequently in the environments of sports and business, **visualization** has shown to help with increasing positive results. In the realm of public speaking, try to draw a mental picture of what your presentation should look like to the audience. Use imagery to see yourself giving a successful speech.

Recognizing the Mind's Role in your Anxiety*:

Examples of mind games that may interfere with your ability to give a good presentation and ideas for eliminating these patterns are listed below:

Mind Game	What It Means	Example	Cognitive Correction
If I am not the best, then I have failed.	When your presentation is seen in black and white terms; it is either perfect or it is a failure.	If your presentation falls short of perfect, you see yourself and the presentation as a total failure.	Always remember that there is no "perfect" presentation. Instead, focus on what went well. Don't criticize yourself too harshly.
Once a failure, always a failure.	When a single poor speech is seen as a never-ending pattern of failure, doomed to repeat itself.	After delivering one poor speech you assume every other speech you will present will also be unsuccessful.	Remind yourself that giving one poor speech does not automatically mean future speeches go the same way.
Assuming the worst	Feeling negative about a presentation without knowing how you really did—you didn't see it.	Assuming that you failed your speech, although you actually received a decent grade.	Always "wait and see" before assuming anything concerning your grade.
Negative Forecasting	A tendency to predict that the speech will go badly, no matter how much preparation and practice you have accomplished.	You predict a week before your speech is to be delivered that you will "stink", despite the fact that you have practiced the speech in front of others numerous times.	NEVER underestimate the effectiveness of proper preparation, daily rehearsal and POSITIVE thoughts.
Catastrophizing	Blowing things out of proportion.	I earned a "C" on the last speech and the next one is tougher so I'll probably get a "D" on that one.	What's the worst that could happen? You could fail the class, true but if that's the worst thing that happens in your life, you've had a VERY GOOD life. Contextualize your speech in the larger picture of life.

* This chart was originally developed by Eric Moreau, professor at CCSN.

EXERCISE 1

CHARTING YOUR COMMUNICATION ANXIETY

Most speakers face a level of anxiety prior to or when engaged in public speaking. Following the steps discussed in your class or in your reading should help reduce the level of anxiety to a manageable level. With practice, and by giving speeches in class you should find that your level of nervousness decreases. *Use the chart below before and after each of your speeches to measure you level of anxiety. Describe how you feel physically and mentally. Finally, circle the number describing your overall anxiety (1 is low and 9 is high).*

	Before the speech I felt	**After the speech I felt**
Speech #1	Overall anxiety 1 2 3 4 5 6 7 8 9	Overall anxiety 1 2 3 4 5 6 7 8 9
Speech #2	Overall anxiety 1 2 3 4 5 6 7 8 9	Overall anxiety 1 2 3 4 5 6 7 8 9
Speech #3	Overall anxiety 1 2 3 4 5 6 7 8 9	Overall anxiety 1 2 3 4 5 6 7 8 9
Speech #4	Overall anxiety 1 2 3 4 5 6 7 8 9	Overall anxiety 1 2 3 4 5 6 7 8 9
Speech #5	Overall anxiety 1 2 3 4 5 6 7 8 9	Overall anxiety 1 2 3 4 5 6 7 8 9

Did your level of anxiety increase or decrease as your gained public speaking experience?

_____

_____

_____

_____

Did you find any particular techniques helpful in managing your communication anxiety?

_____

_____

_____

_____

What suggestions would you give others regarding how to better manage their communication anxiety?

_____

_____

_____

_____

3 *Ethical Public Speaking*

Terms to Know

- Ethics
- Platonic/Absolute Truth
- Sophists
- Dogmatism
- Aristotelian/relative truth
- Ethnocentrism
- Aristotelian proofs
- Ethos
- Logos
- Pathos

Public speaking, whether you are comfortable with it or not, places you in a position of power. As a speaker you are in a unique position to influence your audience's thoughts, to engage them in important and perhaps controversial issues and possibly to motivate them to action. Consequently, you have certain responsibilities that require you to address issues of ethics. **Ethics** can be defined as the study of human moral conduct or the branch of philosophy that address questions of right and wrong in human interaction. As a speaker, you have an ethical responsibility to both yourself and your audience. But was does this ethical responsibility imply? Moreover, how is ethical behavior defined?

Perhaps the most common answer to this question is simply this: Ethical speaking behavior means you are honest in what you say and that you tell the truth. This answer sounds clear and straightforward, yet is far more complex than it appears. At the root of this complexity lies another definition, that of truth. Before you can tell the truth in your presentations, you must first understand how truth can be defined. Key to this understanding is the distinction that must be made between absolute Truth and relative truth.

17

What is truth?

Absolute Truth, as set forth by Plato, holds that truth is complete and unqualified. In other words, **Platonic Truth** defines truth as objective and without question. You may have noticed that truth has been signified above by the use of a capital "T." This is a rhetorical strategy that indicates the immovable position of truth as understood by Plato. Moreover, Plato believed that the understanding and recognition of truth was not available to all; rather, it was solely the province of philosophers who were more equipped to both discover and articulate truth. In fairness to Plato, this approach to truth was largely a product of his time. In his definition of truth, Plato was responding to the **Sophists**, or men who traveled the Greek countryside catering their philosophical message to the specific desires of their paying audiences. Plato found this practice abhorrent because he did not see truth as changeable and open to the highest bidder. Subsequently, he sought to define truth more rigidly.

Relative truth, on the other hand, holds that truth is subjective and open to interpretation. This approach, as advocated by Aristotle, is in direct opposition to Plato's philosophy. **Aristotelian truth**, indicated here by a lower-case "t," defines truth as comparative and qualified, that is to say, open to discussion and dependant on individual environment. Consequently, Aristotle believed that is was possible to disagree on the meaning of truth. While Aristotle largely assumed truth to be open for discussion, he still held that this discussion was largely the territory of philosophers who were trained in such matters.

The contemporary application of this theory, however, can be linked to our understanding of culturally learned norms. More specifically, it can be said that every culture has its own understanding and definition of truth. For example, despite cultural differences, virtually every culture has broadly defined universal approaches to acceptable human behavior. Specifically, every culture has consequences for the unlawful taking of a life, the unlawful taking of property and the unlawful violation of the incest taboo. While at first glance it may appear that cultures then have a shared understanding of truth, the key to understanding their differences lies in the specific cultural definition of *unlawful*. What one culture defines as unlawful, and thus, punishable behavior another culture may define as not only acceptable, but desired behavior. For example, in most of the United States it is unlawful to marry your first cousin. Even in states that allow this practice, it is widely considered by most of society to be an improper violation of the incest taboo. However, in many Arabic and Indian cultures, it has been traditionally held that marriage to a first cousin represents the best possible union.

Every individual operates within both of these definitions of truth. In other words, each of us applies the ideas of both absolute Truth and relative truth to our lives. There are certain issues on which we are immovable. This **dogmatism**, or rigidity of belief, affects everyone. Despite the existence of cultural differences and relativity, each of us has specific beliefs that are not open for discussion. A good example of this is religion. If you were raised in a particular religion and still practice that faith today, you most likely hold that your religion is the most true, that its truth is absolute. Other individuals raised in different religious traditions believe the same thing, despite the fact that their faith differs from yours.

We also operate our lives according to the application of relative truth. There are certain beliefs that we have that have dramatically changed over time and as the direct result of new and varied experiences. These beliefs can be seen as malleable, or impressionable. These kinds of beliefs, or truths, may change throughout our lives, often based on new scientific discovery. For example, for centuries it was believed, absolutely, that the earth was flat. To dispute this belief was to face ridicule and be branded a heretic. However, this belief has since changed. The majority of people on earth do not question the veracity that the earth is round. However, there exists a small group of individuals that see this truth as open for discussion. This group, known and the Flat Earth Society, holds that the earth is indeed flat, as was once believed. They further argue that the contemporary belief that the earth is round is the product of governmental conspiracy, a hoax.

This example, while extreme, illustrates that truth is never just one thing. Consequently, the ethical responsibility to "tell the truth" becomes a more difficult task than it initially appears. The key to recognizing the varied approaches to truth that your audience may have is to simply recognize that these differences exist. The best way to do this is to try your best to avoid **ethnocentrism**, or the belief that your culture and your beliefs are superior to all others. This is an important first step to becoming an ethical speaker, but what else can and should you do to further develop an ethical practice to public speaking?

Putting Ethics into Practice

The term "ethics" comes from the Greek word ethos. **Ethos**, defined as "character," refers to a speaker's perceived credibility by the audience. But what does it mean to be credible? Aristotle argued that a speaker with good credibility demonstrated three things to the audience: good moral character, competence and goodwill. This approach to credibility and public speaking, while roughly 2, 500 years old, still has modern day application. Contemporary scholars have argued that audiences today place the same kind of demands on the speaker. Specifically, audiences identify speakers to be trustworthy when they demonstrate a solid understanding of their subject, illustrate clear reasoning and genuinely seem to care about their audiences. Coincidentally, these concerns also echo Aristotle's idea of proof.

Aristotelian proofs are methods of persuasion that should be used by speakers to strengthen their arguments. However, do not make the mistake of thinking that these proofs should only be used specifically for persuasive speaking. *Every* time you give a speech you are advocating a specific position. You may not be overtly trying to change your audience's beliefs or motivate them to action as a classic persuasive speech does, but you are presenting a particular point of view that you want the audience to understand. It matters little if you are introducing someone or something, informing your audience about a new topic, telling a story or crafting an impromptu speech. Your audience still needs to hear a coherent and ethical presentation. To that end, it is a good idea to include the three Aristotelian proofs in every speech you give. These proofs, identified as **ethos**, **logos**, and **pathos**, strengthen your position as a speaker and help to meet the ethical requirements for public speaking.

Ethos, as defined above, is a speaker's credibility. Speakers that seem honest have a greater impact on their audience. **Logos** can be defined as the logical development of ideas and the clear adherence to structure. Audiences that can easily follow a speaker's argument are more likely to retain his or her message. Subsequent chapters in this book will outline specifically how this structure should be created and articulated. **Pathos** is understood to be an appeal to an audience's sense of emotion. A good speaker not only seems credible and follows structure; he or she must also create an emotional connection to the audience. While it is important to create an emotional appeal you your audience, according to Aristotle, it must be based on sound reasoning. Blatantly manipulating your audience by unfairly playing on fear and anxiety is an unethical use of pathos. For this reason, Aristotle also argued that a speaker must use all three of these proofs to be ethically successful.

Another way to incorporate ethics into your speech is to use your supporting material responsibility. In subsequent chapters you will learn not only what defines ethical research, but also how to ethically incorporate your research into your speech. That said, it is worthwhile to present some brief guidelines here. First and foremost, you must avoid plagiarism and clearly cite your sources in your speech. This means that not only should you properly credit direct quotations, but also paraphrased material and general ideas and theories about your topic that you only learned about through sources other than your own knowledge and experience. A good rule of thumb is if you would cite a source in a written paper, you must also acknowledge it in a verbal presentation. You will not include the complete bibliographic information in your speech, however. Usually the source (person, title of book, title of magazine, etc.) and the date are sufficient. As you will later learn, a complete bibliography should be included in a formal outline.

Additional Tips for Ethical Speaking

- Avoid ethnocentrism. Realize that your audience may have conflicting beliefs that should nevertheless be respected.
- Realize that you do have freedom of speech, but that does not guarantee freedom from consequence.
- Avoid discriminatory language and hate speech. Attack arguments in your speeches, not individuals.
- Incorporate ethos, logos and pathos into your speech. Be sure to use all three of these Aristotelian proofs.
- Be honest in your application of supporting material. Do not manipulate research to make a stronger argument.
- Credit your sources. Do not plagiarize material. When in doubt, use a source citation.
- Be prepared for each speech. Take the necessary time not only to develop your speech, but to practice it as well.

EXERCISES

1) Does the end justify the means? Read the following scenario with your classmates and discuss why the speaker behaved the way he or she did. Is this behavior ever justified?

   A speaker for a global famine relief organization deliberately exaggerates statistics on child hunger in a presentation to potential donors. The speaker believes that by directly appealing to the audience's sense of morality and perhaps pity, more money will be raised and more children will be helped. Is this the right choice given the speaker's commitment to the greater good?

2) After each speech, assess your performance as an ethical speaker using the following checklist.
   - Did your speech respect the values of your audience?
   - Were you honest in your preparation and presentation of your speech?
   - Did you use sound evidence and reasoning?
   - Did you avoid manipulating the emotions of your audience?
   - Did you try to avoid expressions of ethnocentrism and prejudice?

   (Adapted from O'Hair, D., R. Steward and H. Rubenstein. *A Speaker's Guidebook* (Boston: Beford/St. Martin's, 2001) 52.

3) Ethics and ethical speaking are not just confined to the classroom environment. Think about how you would *realistically* act in the various social settings. What does your behavior say about your own code of ethics?
   - You are at a party and hear someone telling an obviously racist joke. What do you do? Laugh? Ignore it? Stay silent, but comment to a friend later?
   - After a day of hearing speeches you are talking with a classmate as you leave the classroom. This person comments on how well they think they did on their speech given that they didn't do any research and fabricated all their source citations. How do you react to this information? Would you take any kind of action?
   - You see a job advertisement for a position that pays well and would be a boost to your career. You know that with some creative tweaking of your resume you could probably get an interview. What do you do?

4 *Listening*

Listening is a vital part of the communication process. As audience members you will spend much more time listening to speakers in the classroom than you will spend giving speeches. To become better critical listeners it is imperative that you recognize that listening is an *active* process, one that requires both concentration and focus. Listening is not merely the act of hearing, but of processing the material that you hear.

However, good, critical listening does not come easy. As this chapter will explore, people choose to selectively listen to speakers based on a variety of factors. Audience members pay attention to what they define as important. This decision is influenced by individual backgrounds and experiences. People also choose to sort and filter information on the basis of what is already familiar to them. Moreover, some listeners are so busy formulating a response to the speaker that they miss much of the speaker's presentation. Instead of taking time to listen, they are instead, waiting for their turn to talk.

Four Types of Listening

There are a variety of listening behaviors that you employ on a daily basis. Each one of these listening behaviors is best suited to a particular environment or context. Knowing the types of listening you participate in as well as the expectations for listening behavior can help prepare you to become a better listener, regardless of the circumstance.

1. **Appreciative:** Appreciative listening is listening simply for pleasure. An excellent example of this type of listening is listening to music. You enjoy the music even if you aren't quite sure what the lyrics are. You may find yourself cranking up the radio to sing along to your favorite song knowing full well that the words you are singing out loud, aren't the actual words of the song. Still, you enjoy the music. In other words, you don't have to completely understand the communicative message to engage in this type of listening. Although you go through a selective process in choosing what you listen to, the intellectual demands placed on you are minimal.

2. **Empathic:** Empathic listening is listening to provide emotional support. An excellent example of this type of listening is when a friend or family member comes to you for feedback usually regarding a personal issue. As a listener you are expected to be supportive and possibly provide advice. However, it is generally not expected that you completely understand the situation before doing so. If a friend comes to you distraught over a recent break-up how are you expected to act? Do you question what went wrong? Possibly. Do you ask if there is anything you can do? Maybe. Do you offer statements that make your friend feel better, perhaps something along the lines of "you're better off without him/her anyway." Most likely. However, do you patiently listen to why the break-up occurred and then pointedly say, "You know, I think your boyfriend/girlfriend has a point." Absolutely not. To do so would violate the expectations of empathic listening.

3. **Comprehensive:** Comprehensive listening is listening to understand. This is the first type of listening behavior to explicitly demand focus and concentration. This is the type of listening that you should be engaged in as a student in the classroom. This very active type of listening requires you to suspend judgment regarding the speaker and his or her topic so that you may fully understand the message. For most audience members, this is a difficult thing to accomplish. Most of us decide in the first thirty seconds or so (if not sooner) of a speaker's presentation whether or not he or she is worth listening to. We make this decision based on a variety of factors such as the speaker's appearance, topic choice, and method of delivery. However, if you let issues such as these prevent comprehensive listening you will most likely miss significant portions of the speaker's argument. It is vital that you try your best to understand what is being said before you either accept or reject it.

4. **Critical:** Critical listening is listening to provide evaluation. This type of listening should only occur once you understand the speaker's argument. However, as noted above, most listeners decide to accept or reject a speaker's ideas often before the speaker has finished his or her introduction. Once again, you must suspend judgment and wait until the speech is over before coming to conclusions regarding either the speaker or the presentation. There is nothing wrong about taking a position or evaluating a speaker's presentation. However, you must wait until you understand the message thoroughly before you do so. In a sense, you must make an informed evaluation of speaker. How can you decide whether or not a speech delivers what it should if you do not give the speaker the courtesy listening to the entire presentation? In short, you can't. Think of it this way: would you want your instructor to listen only to the introduction of your speech and then immediately decide what grade you earned for your presentation? Probably not.

Barriers to Critical Listening

Despite the fact that we recognize the importance of being good, critical listeners, very few of us actually succeed in doing so. Why? If this is such an important component of the communication process, why do so many of us fail at it? Before we attach blame to the myriad of factors responsible for lazy and unfocused listening, it is important to realize that poor listening skills are not entirely your fault. Think about it: your brain can process information far faster than a speaker can present it. Consequently, as a listener you have "gap time" between your ability to handle information and the speaker's ability to communicate it. However, it is your responsibility to use this gap time constructively, to keep your focus and concentration even though the speaker needs adequate time to present his or her ideas. That said, there are also a plethora of factors that interfere with your ability to be a good, critical listener.

1. **External:** External distractions can make critical listening difficult. These distractions are things like noises outside (or inside) the classroom, an unusually warm or cold speaking environment, and audience members either leaving or entering the classroom during a speech, a nearly unforgivable transgression. NEVER do this except in the case of a true emergency. In short, external listening distractions are factors that are outside of your immediate control. All of these instances can interfere with your ability to concentrate on a speaker's message. You must try your best to ignore them and keep your focus where it belongs: on the speaker!

2. **Internal:** Internal distractions are far more likely to interrupt your listening behavior because they originate with your own thoughts and feelings. Internal distractions can be divided into two categories: physiological and psychological. **Physiological distractions** include things like being hungry or sleepy, feeling sick to your stomach or battling a cold and possibly feeling nervous about the speech you are giving that same day. While physiological distractions can be frustrating, they are more easily overcome. Taking precautions like eating, getting enough rest, and utilizing the methods for reducing communication apprehension discussed earlier can greatly minimize the impact of physiological listening distractions.

   Psychological distractions are far more troubling because they encompass a much larger territory. This category of listening distraction is particularly pervasive because it, quite literally, includes everything that you can think of. Distractions ranging from thinking about your personal life to daydreaming about somewhere else you would rather be to planning your weekend are all examples of this type of listening obstacle. Two larger concerns regarding internal barriers to critical listening are the concepts of filtering and trigger words.

Filtering

Filtering refers to the fact that you do not process everything that you hear. In reality, you selectively choose what you remember and what you ignore. This is generally not a conscious process. Although you can certainly choose what to pay attention to and what to disregard, in most cases you make this decision based on your personal and cultural experiences and are not always aware of your listening choices. Consequently, you will automatically be interested in some topics and disinterested in others. For example, if you grew up practicing Islam chances are if a speaker chooses to explain it in a speech your interest will piqued. You will be more likely to pay attention because the speaker is addressing an issue that both interests and impacts you. However, if you know next to nothing about this religious faith you are more likely to either dismiss the topic entirely or jump to the conclusion that you already understand it based on specific (and often inaccurate) media representations.

But how are these preferences shaped? First and foremost, by your acquisition of language. The language you learn to speak both frames and limits your ability to understand the world around you. This linguistic theory, known as the **Sapir-Whorf hypothesis**, holds that the language you speak determines the way you will interpret the world around you. Communication theorist Kenneth Burke advances this same argument of linguistic determinism through his discussion of **terministic screens**. According to Burke, terministic screens refers to the argument that we come to see the world as our symbol systems enable us to see it. For example, in English there exists one word for corner. Yet in Spanish, there are two words that convey the same idea, but with greater precision. *Esquina* indicates an outer corner, as in the corner of a table while *rincón* indicates an inner corner, as in the corner of a room. We can certainly explain these concepts in English, but must use modifiers to do so. We are limited in our expression of these concepts by the words we have been given to describe them. This is true of every language.

The link that can be made to listening behavior should be obvious. Much as we are limited by language in the way we see and understand the world, we are also restricted by our own experiences and perceptions. Moreover, when listening to new and possibly unfamiliar material, we have a tendency to attempt to categorize it, to drag it into something we already understand. French anthropologist Claude Levi-Strauss refers to this very human tendency as the science of the concrete.

Science of the Concrete

The **science of the concrete** conveys the idea that human beings have an innate need to name the unfamiliar. When we hear something new we tend to compare and contrast it to things we have already experienced. If we can satisfactorily compare it to something that is already known we have successfully categorized and thus, made sense of this new material. For example, think about the last time you tried something new and unfamiliar to eat. People that have tried food as varied as rattlesnake, alligator and frog legs all pronounce the same thing: it tastes like chicken! Why this comparison? Because for most people, chicken is a familiar and easily identified taste. When new experiences briefly confound us, we make sense of them by comparing them to things we already know. Conversely, when we experience something new and lack a good analogy to explain it, we must "create a new file," so to speak. Consequently, our bank of experiences grows. Given this reality, our filtering mechanisms, our terministic screens, change and expand in direct correlation to the experiences we have. Think about it: the thoughts and opinions you held as a child are most likely different from the way you think now. Why? Simply because every experience you have creates space for new interpretations to occur. The end result of this process is that you become poised to become a better listener because your available filters have grown.

Trigger Words

Trigger words are words that carry a particular **connotative** meaning for you. In other words, certain words can have either a negative or positive emotional meaning based on your experience, beliefs and values. This is different from the **denotative** meaning of the word which is its generally accepted dictionary definition. The emotional responses created by connotative meaning can easily prevent you from being able or even wanting to listen to the speaker. For example, several semesters ago a COM 101 student gave an informative speech on her family's business of dog breeding. This business had been in her family for generations. Consequently, she was extremely familiar and comfortable with the terminology used in this environment. As a result, in her speech she actually said the phrase, "So when the bitch is ready..." You can imagine the audience reaction. Most people in her audience gasped as if to say, "I can't believe she just said that," and promptly laughed. Why did this reaction occur? Primarily because the connotative meaning of the word overtook its denotative meaning. Although the speaker was referring to the breeding process of dogs and the use of the term "bitch" was entirely appropriate to indicate a female dog in heat, the larger emotional meaning was what the audience responded to. But why was this a problem? Largely because during that moment of laughter and the aftermath that it triggered, the audience was distracted and unable to critically listen to the speaker.

As you can see, trigger words can greatly interfere with an audience's ability to stay focused. These trigger words can be personal, i.e. words that individuals respond to based on their own experiences, or societal, i.e. words that have gained a strong and shared connotative meaning on a collective level. For example, if a speaker is giving a speech advocating the benefits of joining a gym you may start thinking of the last time you worked out, how much it might cost to join a gym or the nearest gym to your home. All of these thoughts are examples of personal triggers. However, the example used above regarding the term "bitch" can be classified as a societal trigger word because its connotative meaning is largely shared by most members of society. According to rhetorician Richard Weaver, certain societal trigger words have gained such power that they act as automatic moral triggers, creating strong emotional and visceral responses in listeners.

These terms, which Weaver referred to as **God and Devil terms**, can motivate listeners to automatically accept or reject a speaker's message, regardless of their ability to truly understand the message. This is what makes God and Devil terms so dangerous and such a threat to critical listening. God terms refer to words that carry the greatest blessing or good that a culture can create. Consequently, they have the power to demand sacrifice often without logical argument. A good example of a God term in larger American culture is the word *freedom*. In our current political climate politicians often talk of "evil-doers" that threaten American freedom. Such a charge, whether it is true or not, plays on our fears that one of our most sacred ideals, freedom, is in jeopardy. As a result, as listeners we become emotionally motivated to act, often foregoing the critical reasoning that should frame our action. This is not to say that emotional appeals are never appropriate; however, speakers that make emotional appeals in lieu of logical argument are taking an unethical shortcut. As audience members you must be aware that this rhetorical strategy severely hampers your ability to listen critically and comprehensively.

In opposition to God terms are Devil terms. These terms function in virtually the same way, but are terms of repulsion and the greatest evils in a culture. A good example of a Devil term in larger American society is illustrated by the historical reality of McCarthyism. In the United States, in the 1950s, the term *communist* was understood as a devil term. It represented everything America defined itself against. The mere act of accusing someone of affiliating with this political party was enough to pronounce that person's guilt. More contemporary examples include terms like *terrorism*, *Nazi*, *Al Qaeda*, and still, *communism*.

Tips for Improving Listening Skills

Although listening is an incredibly important part of the communication process, as you can see, it does not come easily. The following list offers brief suggestions for improving and enhancing your own listening behaviors.

- First realize that you have your own biases and prejudices. Before you can become a good listener, you must first realize you need improvement. Don't worry, *everyone* can and should improve their listening skills.
- Suspend judgment. Before evaluating a speaker's presentation make sure that you understand it. Make an evaluation, but only after you have listened to the speech in its entirety.
- Follow the speaker's argument. Knowing how a good speech is structured gives you a tool to understand where the speaker is going. Look for the components of structure that a good speaker should be following.
- Look for evidence. Listen carefully to see that the speaker supports his or her claims.

- Empathize with the speaker. Trying to understand where the speaker is coming from can make listening a more enjoyable process.
- Be aware of distractions. As listeners we all get distracted. This is unavoidable. It is how we react to these distractions that determine our success as listeners. Try to stay focused and concentrate on the speaker's message.

EXERCISES

1) Consider the word *feminist*. Working in small groups and putting your personal feelings about this term aside, think about how it is portrayed in the dominant culture of the United States. In order to do this, list as many adjectives as possible to describe this term as it is largely understood in media representation. Again, you are not writing down how you personally feel about this term; rather, you are identifying how the larger culture defines it. Look at your list. How many of the adjectives on your list are positive? Negative? Do you think this term meets Weaver's definition for a Devil term? Why or why not?

2) Think about the following list of words/topics that you might hear in a speech class. How do you feel about them? Do you form an opinion based simply on your emotional response? We all react emotionally to some people and topics, but good critical listeners are able to keep their emotions in check while listening to and evaluating a speaker. **Remember, to be a good listener you must suspend judgment, empathize with the speaker and try to see the topic from his or her point of view. Critical listening takes work!**

	Positive	Negative	Neutral
1. Martha Stewart			
2. Barry Bonds			
3. President George W. Bush			
4. President Bill Clinton			
5. Tupac			
6. Britney Spears			
7. Marijuana			
8. Terrorism			
9. Michael Jackson			
10. Democrat			
11. Republican			
12. Liberal			
13. Conservative			
14. Same-sex marriage			
15. Capital punishment			

3) Think about your own listening behaviors. What are some of your strengths? Weaknesses? How do you think you can improve your listening skills? In a brief paragraph, create your own personal listening objectives outlining how you want to improve as a listener during the course of the semester.

5 *Audience Diversity and Audience Analysis*

Terms to Know

- Audience Adaptation
- Perception
- Idioms
- Egocentrism
- Maslow's Hierarchy of Needs
- Audience Demographics
- Audience Profile
- Audience Survey
- Environmental Analysis
- Audience Adaptation

As a speaker, it should come as no surprise that your primary goal is for your audience to retain and remember your message. But how do you create a message that appeals to the diverse audiences you will inherently encounter? The answer to this question is twofold. First, you must recognize and learn to appreciate the diversity that will be present in your audience. Second, you must gather as much information about your audience as possible so that you may craft a presentation that speaks to their interests and desires. This rhetorical strategy is known as **audience adaptation**, or your ability to modify your message to meet the needs of your listeners.

Audience Diversity

Every audience you encounter as a speaker will be diverse to some degree. You may have individuals who vary in age, cultural background, religion, ethnicity, socio-economic position, etc. However, even with audiences that seem to be of comparable background on the surface, diversity is found beneath the veneer of similarity. This diversity is primarily reflected in the varied perceptions your audiences may have about the same topic. To some extent this argument is a continuation of the filtering process we undergo as audience members that was discussed in the listening chapter. However, it is worthwhile to explore this idea again because the focus shifts from what the *listener* should do to what the *speaker* must do to address these varied and diverse audience perceptions.

Perception can be defined as the process of selecting, organizing, and interpreting sensory data in a way that enables us to make sense of our world. It certainly should come as no surprise that individuals process and interpret experiences differently. Thus, perception becomes highly subjective. We make selections regarding meaning based on our cultural background, our own experience, our age our gender, etc. Therefore, what one person sees, another cannot. A good way to illustrate this phenomenon is to take a look at the following picture. Many of you have probably seen this image before. What are you looking at? An old woman or a young woman? The image is the same, yet each individual will process the picture differently. If you try hard, you should be able to identify both the old woman and the young girl, but one will undoubtedly be easier for you to see. Take a look:

What do you see when you look at this image?

An old woman or young girl?

If you are having difficultly seeing both images, here is a hint: the old woman's nose is the young woman's chin. Why is one image easier for you to identify? The answer is complex, created by everything that composes who you are. Irish novelist Elizabeth Bowen has said "No object is mysterious. The mystery is in your eye." This sentiment is a perfect companion to the idea of perception as well as audience diversity. Each member of your audience will approach and understand your topic differently. It is your responsibility as a speaker to try and understand those differences *before* you give your speech in order to adapt to your individual audience needs.

Compounding the reality of perceptual differences in your audience is the fact that differences in perception occur both in what your audience hears and what your audience sees. In short, audience members will respond differently to both your verbal and nonverbal messages. It may seem strange to address verbal message confusion in a strictly English language public speaking course, but as you recall from the listening chapter, audience members are often triggered by their own connotative meanings. Moreover, given the diversity found within a typical CCSN classroom, it is unwise to assume that everyone in your audience learned English as their primary language or speaks English the same way that you do. Many of your classmates are bilingual, from different regions of the United States or international students representing a wide variety of foreign countries. As such, you need to strive to be as clear as you can in delivering your message to them. In subsequent chapters the importance of clear language use will be discussed, but for now, know that it is necessary for audience adaptation. Briefly consider the following example:

What's in a Word? Everything

Each workday morning, several moms on the block drop off their toddlers with their Colombian baby-sitter, who takes excellent care of the children. One afternoon, the sitter's 13-year-old son, Ernesto, accompanies her as she walks the children back to their homes. When they arrive at Isa's house, her father, Fred, greets them. It is the first time he has met Ernesto.

In halting English, Ernesto says, "Your daughter is very beautiful." Fred thanks him. Ernesto replies, "*No molesta*." Then when he sees his daughter kiss Ernesto goodbye, Fred becomes enraged.

What went wrong?

With heightened consciousness about sexual abuse, Fred had jumped to the conclusion that Ernesto's statement meant "I didn't molest her." Although Fred's wife challenged her husband's Spanish-language skills, he insisted that he understood Spanish very well.

However, when his wife later related the incident to the other parents, one of the other fathers roared with laughter when he heard Ernesto's exact words. This man, from Puerto Rico, then explained that in Spanish, *molestar*, also means "to disturb." All that Ernesto was trying to tell Fred about his daughter was that "She's no trouble." There was no hint of sexual abuse.

Rule: Even though a word in another language may be similar to one in English, it may have a completely different meaning.

Source

Dresser, N. "What's in a Word? Everything," *The Los Angeles Times* (9 January, 1995) B4.

It is also worthwhile to point out that given the diversity of your audience and the plethora of perceptions they may have it unwise to rely on idiomatic expressions to carry your message. Idiomatic expressions, or **idioms**, are phrases that carry peculiar meaning for a particular culture. They are extremely difficult for non-native speakers to understand because they cannot be translated literally. Consider the following phrases that are quite common in American English:

1. *"See ya later."* To native speakers this phrase often stands in for "goodbye" and simply means you will see the person you are talking to at some unspecified later date. However, to a non-native speaker this phrase indicates a need to schedule a definite future contact.

2. *"We must act on this ASAP."* Native speakers understand that ASAP is an acronym for "as soon as possible." However, many non-native speakers have no idea what the speaker is saying.

3. *"We need to cover all bases."* This baseball analogy makes perfect sense to native speakers. When we hear this we know that all details and possible scenarios need to be accounted for. However, non-native speakers are often confused by the literal translation and assume that a blanket is needed to actually cover something.

All languages have these problems when it comes to translation. American English speakers have no trouble understanding phrases like "to laugh one's head off" or "to be down in the dumps." But if English speakers heard these sentiments expressed in French, their respective equivalents would be *Se fendre la pêche* or "to split one's peach" and *Avoir le cafard* or "to have the cockroach." Would non-native French speakers be able to easily understand these phrases? Most decidedly not.

The impact this language diversity has on audience analysis is this: you must not assume that everyone in your audience will automatically understand you. When possible, you must consider the make-up of your listeners and attempt to modify your message when necessary so that as many people as possible will understand and remember your message. When you disregard language diversity and more importantly, diversity in perception and meaning, your lose part of your intended audience. Consider the now infamous example of General Motors attempting to market and sell their Chevy Nova in Central and South America. In Spanish *no va* translates into "doesn't go." What kind of a name for a car is that? With a bit of audience analysis and adaptation, this marketing campaign would have been much more successful. Not only can perceptions regarding verbal messages impede your success as a public speaker, so can nonverbal misunderstandings. Take a look at the following innocent mistake.

Meal Runs Afoul of Taiwan Custom

Kwang-Fu, newly arrived from Taiwan, moves in with the Quinn family to learn English. The first day, he warms a metal pot in the microwave oven and overloads the washing machine. Kindly, his hosts caution him to ask for instructions before using the appliances.

On Sunday, Mrs. Quinn prepares a special family meal. She places a beautifully roasted chicken in front of him, but notices that he only seems to pick at the food. She asks, "Didn't you enjoy my cooking?"

He answers, "Yes, it was delicious, and I will leave here just as soon as I find another place to live." Mrs. Quinn is dumbfounded.

What went wrong?

Incredulous, Mrs. Quinn asked Kwang-Fu why he wanted to move. He explained that in Taiwan, when a person is not welcome, the host places a chicken with its head facing the unwanted party. Mrs. Quinn had placed the chicken in front of Kwang-Fu with the neck cavity facing him. He interpreted this as her request for him to leave. Mrs. Quinn reassured him that this was not an American custom.

During a New Year's meal, a Taiwanese boss may inform an employee he wishes to fire him by facing a chicken toward the unfortunate worker. If no one is to be fired, the boss faces the bird toward himself.

Rule: Placement of food on the table can have multiple interpretations.

Source

Dresser, N. "Meal Runs Afoul of Taiwan Custom," *The Los Angeles Times* (22 August, 1994) B5.

In the above example, Mrs. Quinn illustrates positive behavior because she attempts to understand the root of the confusion and takes steps to further explain herself so that her intentions are clear. This is a lesson that can be learned by public speakers as well. How you carry yourself, the gestures you make, the eye contact you give and the facial expressions you use all convey a meaning to your audience. Sometimes you are unaware of the impact you may be having on your audience. While it is true that most audience analysis and adaptation occurs before and perhaps during your speech, do not discount the possibility that you may need to clarify your message after you have concluded your speech. This can happen during an official question and answer period or, more likely, in informal conversation with your classmates.

So far, much time as been spent understanding the diverse perceptions that you will most likely encounter with your audience. However, the physical make-up of your audience is equally important. To that end, the next section of this chapter addresses practical methods and tools you can use to learn as much as possible about your audience before you give your speech.

Audience Analysis

Egocentrism refers to the reality that people tend to pay closer attention to topics and issues that directly affect them or reflect their values and beliefs. Audience members want to feel that your speech has something to do with them and are more likely to listen if they feel they have a stake in your topic. For this reason, you should do everything you can to learn what your audience cares about. There are several tools at your disposal to help you with this task. Applying Maslow's Hierarchy of Needs, understanding audience demographics and conducting audience surveys all serve to bridge the gap between your topic and the interests of the audience.

Maslow's Hierarchy of Needs explores the nature of human drives and ambitions. Maslow was a psychologist who studied humans to find out what makes them tick. He concluded that there are 5 stages of needs, and one cannot adequately reach one stage without first fulfilling the needs of the stage before it.

At a base level, we have to get our physical needs met; this means acquiring food, oxygen and water. Without these, you're not likely to be dashing around trying to find your soul mate; you have other matters to take care of first.

Once we have met our physical needs, we then try to ensure that we keep getting those needs met. Here, we attend to safety and security matters. We seek shelter, ensure medical assistance, and getting steady employment, etc.

When we feel our safety and security needs are adequately met, we then go about seeking friendships, relationships, social contacts, etc. After those are fulfilled, we seek to achieve self-esteem and social esteem (e.g., a position with a title and authority).

Finally, at the highest level is self-actualization. In simple terms, this means "be all that you can be." What is your ultimate potential? To be a great writer? Engineer? Speaker? Whatever your fullest potential truly is, this is the level at which you can achieve it.

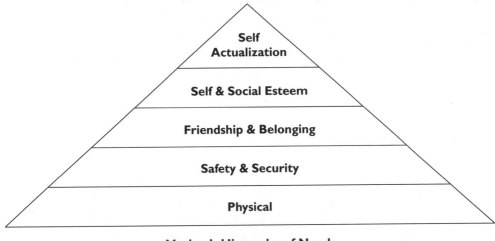

Maslow's Hierarchy of Needs

Knowing that this is at least somewhat how humans think and operate, we can see how it might be applied in the realm of audience analysis. For example, if you're trying to sell a mini-van to a family you're likely to appeal to the need for safety and security. On the other hand, if you're trying to sell a Lexus, you'll probably appeal to the level of self- and social esteem. Always consider your audiences needs and desires through Maslow's Hierarchy of Needs when constructing your arguments.

Audience demographics are categories of membership found within your audience. One way that speakers can approach audience analysis is to examine the basic demographic features of their audience and then weigh the importance of those features to their chosen topic. Common demographic categories can include:

- Age
- Socio-economic status
- Culture
- Religion

- Gender
- Education
- Group affiliations
- Occupation

Each of these categories can indicate a certain predisposition to certain topics. For example, if you want to give an informative speech on the importance of developing a good retirement plan, the demographic of age plays an important role. Chances are you will develop this topic differently for people in their early twenties than for people in their late fifties. This is not to say that age determines interest, but rather that there are different strategies for saving based on how much time you have to accumulate wealth. Again, you would need to weigh the importance of demographic factors. With a topic such as saving for retirement, gender does not make a huge difference. Both women and men need to save for retirement so the gender make-up of your audience matters little with this topic.

Demographic analysis can be a useful tool; however, it should not be sole factor in determining audience adaptation. While there are certain generalities that can be seen in group membership, to rely solely on these generalities is to stereotype. Remember, the most important part of demographic analysis is to *weigh the importance* of specific traits. Do not assume that just because your audience is made up primarily of women, men, Catholics, retirees, blue-collar workers or teachers that they would therefore not be interested in some topics. Use demographic analysis to get a sense of what your audience might like to hear, but do not make this decision absolute. Demographic analysis is a starting point that should be combined with specific data you have gathered about your audience via audience surveys and/or questionnaires.

Audience surveys and **questionnaires** are excellent ways to tailor your concerns about your topic to your individual audience. They allow you to ask specific questions regarding your audience's prior knowledge about your topic, their opinions about it and whether or not they are even interested in learning more. If you have the time and opportunity to do so, consider administering a survey or questionnaire to your audience. This will allow you to more precisely determine how your audience might respond to your topic. Some things to remember:

1. Keep your questions short and to the point.
2. Keep the questionnaire short.
3. Provide room for comments.
4. Keep obvious bias out of the questions so you don't simply get the answers you want.
5. Make the questionnaire anonymous.

One final note regarding audience surveys and questionnaires: Be sure you allow adequate time to conduct a survey before you are scheduled to speak. Based on your audience's responses, you may want or need to make changes. Allow yourself time to do so.

A final issue regarding audience adaptation addresses the concept of **environmental analysis**. This kind of analysis refers to the physical arrangement of the room where you will be speaking. Thinking about the make-up of the room prior to giving your speech can result in a more confident and prepared presentation. Know that you may need to adapt to the environment and practice your speech at home just like you want to give it in front of the classroom. You must consider these elements:

- Physical Arrangement of the Speaking Situation: Are you speaking in front of an audience in a classroom in rows, or a U-shape? Is your audience seated at tables during your presentation at a luncheon? The physical arrangement will impact your delivery.

- Size of the audience: Speaking before an audience of 25 versus 250 will force you to enlist different behaviors. Will you need a microphone for all to hear you? If so, is it a wireless microphone so you have more freedom of movement? Is it a hands-free microphone? How will your eye contact alter based on the audience's size?

- Time of day: Are you speaking at a luncheon? If so are you speaking before, during or after the meal? All situations require different considerations. How will your speech change for a 7A.M. meeting versus one at 6 P.M.?

- Occasion: Your speech about a best friend will differ if it is given at his wedding rather than his funeral. Occasions impact the mood of your presentation.

- Speaking from a podium or not: Knowing whether or not your speech is presented from a podium will impact your movement, eye contact, gestures and interaction with the audience.

Think about the specific changes you made need to make based on the above factors.

EXERCISES

1) Consider the following idiomatic expressions. Although they are all in English, they are not readily understood by Americans. Examine these phrases in small groups and try to identify the meaning behind them.
   a. "a pretty pass" (Great Britain)
   b. "come to heel" (Great Britain)
   c. "have a crow to pluck" (Great Britain)
   d. "to stump up" (Great Britain)
   e. "butter for fat" (The Bahamas)
   f. "cut your grass" (The Bahamas)
   g. "grind somebody up in your heart" (The Bahamas)
   h. "pick somebody's mouth" (The Bahamas)

2) You will be giving several speeches in front of your classmates in the course of the semester. Take some time and answer the following questions about the demographics of your audience and the environmental analysis of your classroom.

Audience Profile Sheet

❏ What is the estimated age range of your audience?

❏ What is the average age of your audience?

❏ What is the gender make-up of your audience?

❏ What is the educational level of this audience?

❏ What "degree majors" are represented in your audience?

❏ What number of the audience members is employed?

❏ What is the socio-economic level of your audience?

❏ What group affiliations do audience members have?

❏ What cultures are represented in your audience?

❏ are the physical arrangements for the speaking situation?

❏ What time of day will you speaking?

❏ What is the size of your audience?

❏ Will you be speaking from a lectern or podium?

3) With an idea of the characteristics of your audience and the environment you can now think about adaptation. Think about how you will adapt to your audience and list the changes you want to make below.

Audience Adaptation Worksheet

Factor	Adaptation needed
Time	
Place	
Physical Arrangement	
Size of Audience	
Age	
Gender	
Educational level	
Socio-economic Level	
Culture	
Group Affiliations	

What is the audience's knowledge of your topic?

_____

_____

_____

What connections to the audience can you make in your introduction?

_____

_____

_____

Have you selected supporting materials that will be credible to the audience?

_____

_____

_____

What adaptations in your language can you make to help the audience understand your message?

_____

_____

_____

6 *Research*

Terms to Know

- Claim
- Evidence
- Research
- Topic selection
- Tree diagramming
- Statistics
- Testimony
- Examples
- Principles
- Emotional appeals
- Personal knowledge
- Library
- Interview
- World Wide Web (WWW)
- URL
- Keywords
- Online databases
- Scholarly research
- Scholarly journals
- Giving attribution (citing)
- Plagiarism
- Bibliography
- Hanging indent
- Works Cited
- Annotated Bibliography

In the chapter on organization, you learn that speeches require **claims**, which are statements you want your audience to understand, remember, and act upon. In general, depending upon the purpose of the speech (informative or persuasive), you'll be spending time either clarifying or supporting each claim that you provide. In order to clarify or support, you'll need to provide some kind of evidence. **Evidence** is information used to clarify or support a claim.

You obtain this evidence through a variety of sources, and you have to evaluate this evidence as well. This process of gathering and interpreting evidence is called **research**. Research is fundamental to any speech making endeavor. It is always dangerous to assume that you know all there is to know about your topic, no matter how skilled and educated you may believe yourself to be. Knowledge evolves, facts change, and new information and ideas are constantly discovered. As such, any savvy speaker will conduct research as part of his or her presentation.

This chapter will explore the fundamental elements of the research process. Specifically, it will look at ways to choose your speech topic, types of evidence to gather for it, ways to evaluate that evidence, sources to explore to find that evidence, and ways to present that evidence through delivery and bibliographies.

Finding Your Topic

Obviously, before you begin gathering data, you need to know the topic of your presentation. In some speaking situations, the topic may be chosen for you. In other situations, you may be given only a very general idea of a topic area, and you'll need to develop a more specific focus without a lot of guidance from others. In public speaking classes, you are very often allowed to determine your own topic, and this can be a very overwhelming decision since there can be so many topics from which to choose.

Nonetheless, there are some approaches to **topic selection** that can assist you:

- *Focus on what you know and what interests you*. Choose topic areas that interest you or about which you've taken coursework and done some learning. You also have to ask yourself how much you already know about the topic. Be honest with yourself.

- *Choose a topic for which you have access to information*. For example, this current chapter focuses on various online databases.

- *Choose topics for which you have time to conduct such research.*

- *Keep in mind your speaking time limit*. How much information can you reasonable fit within the time frame? How much information does your audience need to know? There's nothing wrong with being unable to cover a topic in depth if you have limited time. Instead, explain to your audience that you're focused on what you believe are the most important points in that topic area.

- *Choose a topic that's appropriate to the setting.*

- *Give the audience something NEW*. Whereas you want a topic that's familiar to you, you might consider a topic about which your audience is less likely to be familiar, in order to give them something interesting. If your topic is one about which your audience is probably familiar, then *take a unique angle* on it and focus on some new discovery or innovation in that topic area. You could also try *challenging common perceptions or stereotypes* about it.

- *Search newspapers and magazines for current issues and events*. Current topics are particularly interesting.

- *Search traditional institutional topics* in such areas as the arts, education, government, health, military, science, recreation & leisure, etc.

- *Search research databases, such as Opposing Viewpoints*. You can find instructions for this database in the Appendix. Such databases list a host of topic areas. Note that while Opposing Viewpoints deals with issues and controversies – and, thus, works well for persuasive speeches – it can be useful for informative speeches as well. For instance, you could choose a persuasive topic such as gun control, yet also do an informative speech about gun control in general (e.g., its history, its intended purposes, areas of controversy and agreement, etc.).

- *Consider using **tree diagramming***. This method of working with information is given its name because it "branches out" at new levels of related ideas. Notice that information keeps being broken down, or branched, into new levels. For instance, suppose you're writing a speech about the media. That's a very broad topic, so you might want to break it down into smaller sub-topics, perhaps as follows:

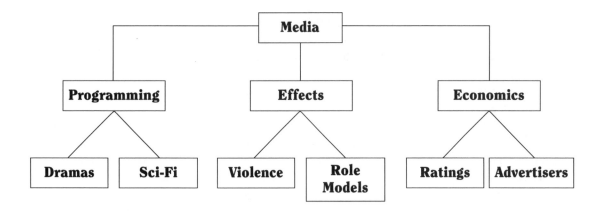

We could, of course, break each level down into further levels. For instance, we could break "Dramas" down into Soap Operas, Police Shows, and Medical Shows. You could choose the topic of your speech at any of these levels and then break it down further still.

You'll find that this method can also be helpful in developing an understanding of outlines. See, also, the chapter on Organizing and Outlining for a further look at tree diagramming.

Types of Evidence

Once you know the topic, you have to gather evidence for it. There are several types of evidence that can be gathered. Each has certain provisions that should be attended to when using them. Five major kinds of evidence that will be explored here include statistics, testimony, examples, principles, and emotional appeals.

Statistics are forms of numerical information that describe some population or event. A very loose definition would suggest that statistics can be any information that involves a number. Consider some of the following types of statistics:

- Raw numbers (e.g., "Last year, we spent $35 million on the project.")
- Central tendencies (e.g., "The average grade on the exam was 75%.")
- Probabilities (e.g., "Smokers are 90% more likely to die of cancer than are non-smokers.")
- Trends (e.g., "At this growth rate, we'll have 40,000 students by 2006.")

Regardless of their form, there are certain characteristics of statistics that you need to attend to when choosing to use them. Ideally, you'll want to take a course in quantitative research to fully understand the nuances of statistics and what they can mean. To give you a flavor for what the nuances are like, consider that people with training in statistics look to such matters as: 1) operational definitions (are the terms of the categories clearly defined); 2) whether all data are reported; 3) whether the base of a percentage is properly estimated; 4) whether representative samples are used; or 5) whether survey questions are constructed fairly; 6) what is the make-up of the population sampled. Unfortunately, this course cannot go into the nuances of research in any particular detail. Certainly, if you're going to work with statistics in your future occupation(s), you'll need to take a research course.

For now, if you're pretty unfamiliar with statistics, there are at least two criteria you can consider when using them. First, you want them to be current unless working with a trend. Current statistics are those that are no more than 2 years old; even then, those could be outdated. You have to consider what you want to use the statistic for.

For instance, if you're trying to convince your audience to legalize euthanasia, and you use a 1985 survey of public attitudes about euthanasia as a source of evidence, it's unlikely you'll be convincing with data that are nearly 20 years old. Attitudes may well have changed in that time. On the other hand, if you want to show a trend in public attitudes, you might want to compare those 1985 results with something more recent to show if or how attitudes have altered.

Second, you want to use statistics that come from a reliable source. Later in this chapter, you'll be introduced to several such sources. For now, realize that many sources, such as web pages, often provide statistical information without also acknowledging the source from which this information was obtained. Anyone can post statistics; it doesn't mean they're true or accurate.

Testimony is a form of evidence that relies on the expertise of others. Do not confuse testimony with your own personal experiences. Certainly, your own expertise in a subject can be brought into play; but here, testimony is referring to the use of some other person, organization, institution, book, etc. to lend expertise and credibility to what you have to say. Testimony could be the spoken or written words of a doctor; something published by an academic institution; a passage from the Koran; etc.

Note that testimony does not have to be a direct quotation, although quotes are clearly acceptable as well. As long as you at least paraphrase your source (and give attribution, which is covered later in this chapter), you are using testimonial evidence.

As with statistics, there are certain criteria associated with the use of testimony to which you need to attend. First, you have to determine if your source is really qualified for the subject matter. (If so, you also have to provide those qualifications in your speech.) Here, you need to ask such questions as whether the source is competent to report information in the subject area (e.g., they may need some kind of degree to be credible); or whether the source would be likely to report information fairly.

For that matter, you also have to consider the audience's perceived credibility of the source. They may find a source to be highly credible that you know is not credible; you may be tempted to use such a source simply to get the audience on your side. Read the chapter on ethics for more guidance in this kind of decision. On the other hand, you may have a source that you know is highly credible but that the audience either will not likely know or not likely respect. Here, you may have to make an extra effort to convince the audience that your source is valuable.

Second, you also want to consider the nature of the source material. For instance, you may want to choose source information that's available to everyone. You also need to consider whether they way you're using your source's information is the way the source intended it to be used. (If not, at least be honest with your audience about what you're doing.)

Finally, consider the consistency of the testimony. Is it consistent with other information that you read or heard in the information source where you found this? Is it consistent with information and evidence that can be found in other sources?

Here, in particular, be careful to differentiate between testimony of fact and testimony of opinion. Testimony of fact is where a source attempts to state some truth that can be proven or disproven with data. Testimony of opinion, however, may be based more on what a source thinks or feels is true or ought to be true. You can't really prove or disprove this kind of testimony; all anyone can do is offer similar or contrary points of view. Regardless, be careful never to treat opinions as facts.

Examples are a third type of evidence. They can include stories, and they can be either real or hypothetical. They involve events, people, or objects that illustrate your claim in a concrete manner.

As an example of an example, suppose you were giving a speech about successful marketing principles. You might draw upon CCSN's steady growth over the past decade to illustrate how these marketing principles work in practice.

You obviously want examples that are clear, specific, and that actually illustrate the point you're trying to make. Research in social psychology has shown that most people find real examples to be more compelling than hypothetical ones. This makes sense, since hypothetical examples are always of a "what if" nature, and someone can always respond by saying "yes, but show me something that really happens."

In many instances, you'll also probably want to make certain that your examples are typical. Here, you're trying to avoid a criticism of "yes, but that happened only once, so it doesn't really illustrate your point." Along these lines, you may want to limit the extent to which you use your own personal experiences and stories as evidence. Too much of their use could make you begin to look self-centered. Excessive use of self-experience can also raise questions as to whether you might be an exception to the rule (i.e., "ya, well, it happened to you, but is this typical of others?").

When using examples, you have to also consider whether you have a sufficient number of them to prove your point or illustrate it clearly. You also need a certain accountability, wherein you should also be able to explain examples that might run contrary to your argument.

A fourth type of evidence is the use of principles. **Principles** could be defined as either some kind of truth or some kind of guideline for behavior. For example, suppose you wanted to argue against the death penalty. There are several types of evidence from which you could choose. Maybe you bring into play statistics that compare the number of murders between states with and without the death penalty. Perhaps you draw upon the testimony of a religious expert who speaks against it. You could also bring in examples of people who were executed for murder but later were proven innocent.

Another approach, however, could be to draw upon the principle of "killing is wrong." This principle is certainly espoused in a variety of religious and ethical doctrines. You could apply your principle to your argument as follows:

1. Most religious and ethical doctrines teach us that killing is wrong.
2. Capital punishment is killing.
3. Therefore, capital punishment is wrong.

This may sound simple enough, but an effective use of principles takes time and practice to master. You may want to limit your search for evidence to statistics, testimony and examples until you become more proficient with principles.

If you wish to use principles, you should at least consider, first, that the principle has to be applicable to the situation you're describing. Also, consider that there can be competing principles for which you need to be accountable. For instance, someone can just as easily counter your capital punishment argument with the principles of "justice" and "an eye for an eye."

Along these lines, you also have to consider that principles are often relative to different cultures and belief systems. What's "true" or "right" to one group of people may well be "false" or "wrong" to another. For instance, there is a cultural called the Yanomami who reside in a very challenging part of the Amazon. Members of the culture need to live life rather aggressively, perhaps even violently by our standards, in order to survive.

Many years ago, an anthropologist went to study the Yanomami. Despite months of effort, they simply would not accept him and tended to constantly harass him. Finally one night, he'd had enough, and in a fit of anger, he went to the river and cut all of their canoes loose. The next morning, the tribe congratulated him on his efforts, since he had (in their eyes) finally demonstrated the necessary attitude that the tribe valued.

Now, in many cultures, we would assume that the tribe would have probably been furious with the anthropologist and punished him severely. Their value system, however, was dramatically different.

As a more current and local example, you might also consider that, shortly after the shooting at Columbine a few years ago, Congress tried to quickly pass legislation that would require the posting of the 10 Commandments in all public schools. Debate in Congress quickly ensued, however, when it was discovered that the 10 Commandments in Christianity are not identical to those in Judaism. What one group of Congresspeople assumed was a universal set of principles turned out to be incorrect.

The point here is that it's dangerous to assume that what you value and hold to be true will be the same for all of your audience members, particularly if you have a fairly diverse audience. You can just as quickly alienate a good portion of your audience by playing to a certain principle as you can garner support with it.

A fifth type of evidence is emotional appeals. **Emotional appeals** are efforts to motivate an audience by stimulating needs and drives, or by drawing upon their values and sentiments. As with principles, emotional appeals can appear to be easy to use, but they also require a considerable amount of skill to be handled adeptly.

For instance, you don't necessarily want to use emotional appeals at the expense of reasoning. Advertising often works at this level. Consider, for instance, the famous claim that some cereal is "part of a nutritious breakfast." So are your cereal bowl and spoon. That doesn't mean that any of these are necessarily nutritious, especially the cereal. The wording in the ad, however, seems to give it a rational-sounding quality.

It might also be worth pondering that, in recent years, we've been introduced to the notion of "emotional intelligence," which refers to the extent to which people are capable of recognizing and managing their emotional states. Research in this area has shown that many business managers, for instance, often make decisions on the basis of how they feel rather than on the basis of actual evidence put before them. Similarly, it may be easy to sway an audience's emotions, but on the ethical side, you have to determine if that's in the best interest of both them and you.

Another way to approach emotional appeals would be to examine audience values and sentiments. Here, we can turn to research by Rieke and Sillars, who identified several predominant types of audience value systems. For example, consider the Puritan value system. For audiences who tend to hold to these kinds of beliefs, they find such values as hard work, thrift, morality, etc. to be positive; likewise, they find such values as laziness, poverty, immorality, etc. to be negative.

If you know your audience is predominantly Puritan in nature, you can appeal to the positive values and speak out against the negative ones, perhaps even using some of these as catch phrases (e.g., "we should all actively work hard in a thrifty manner, dedicating ourselves in selfless sacrifice to the higher virtue of righteousness, which is our duty").

That's a little blatant, but you get the idea. However, if you do not personally come from such a value system, it's probably not wise to pretend to be someone who is; rather, you might acknowledge to the audience that you recognize their values and respect them, and speak about them in this manner.

Audience value systems as identified by Rieke & Sillars

Puritan
(1) <u>Positive:</u> activity, work, thrift, morality, dedication, sacrifice, selflessness, virtue, righteousness, duty, dependability, savings, dignity, law, order
(2) <u>Negative:</u> waste, immorality, infidelity, theft, hunger, poverty, disgrace, vanity

Enlightenment
(1) <u>Positive:</u> freedom, science, nature, rationality, democracy, fact, liberty, individualism, knowledge, intelligence, reason, rights, natural laws, progress
(2) <u>Negative:</u> ignorance, thoughtlessness, error, indecision, irrationality, dictatorship, fascism, falsehood, book burning, regression

Progressive
(1) <u>Positive:</u> practicality, efficiency, change, improvement, science, future, modern, progress, evolution
(2) <u>Negative:</u> old-fashioned, regression, impossible, backward

Transcendental
(1) <u>Positive:</u> humanitarian, individualism, respect, intuition, truth, equality, sympathy, affection, forgiveness, feeling, love, sensitivity, emotion, compassion, brotherhood, friendship
(2) <u>Negative:</u> science, reason, mechanical, hate, war, anger, insensitive, coldness, unemotional, logic

Personal Success
(1) <u>Positive:</u> career, family, friends, recreation, economic security, identity, health, individualism, affection, respect, enjoyment, dignity, consideration, fair play, personal, self
(2) <u>Negative:</u> dullness, routine, hunger, poverty, disgrace, coercion, disease, sickness

Collectivist
(1) <u>Positive:</u> cooperation, joint-action, teamwork, unity, brotherhood, together, social good, social order, humanitarianism, aid and comfort, equality
(2) <u>Negative:</u> disorganization, selfishness, personal greed, inequality, self-centered

---

Five Key Resources for Finding Evidence

Now that you know about different types of evidence and their uses, the question obviously arises as to where to locate this evidence. Numerous sources are available, but five will be examined here: personal knowledge, libraries, interviews, world wide web (WWW) sources, and online databases.

Depending on the speaking circumstances, you may want to consider making limited use of **personal knowledge** unless (1) you have established credentials that qualify you as an "expert" on the subject or (2) the nature of the speech requires you to draw upon your personal knowledge base. It's not that personal knowledge and experiences are somehow bad; but to rely exclusively on these can lead to problems where research may be clearly required. In short, experienced speakers never assume that they know all there is to know about their topic. Knowledge changes, and what you think you know now may well be out of date. For that matter, you audience deserves to have the most up-to-date information made available to them, and there is no substitute for research when it comes to finding such information.

A more traditional starting point is often a **library**, either public or college. For this course, you're best advised to use the CCSN library system. The public libraries have many fine sources of information, but college libraries often have scholarly materials that aren't available in public libraries.

Libraries can provide resources such as books, magazines, newspapers, atlases, dictionaries, encyclopedias, almanacs, and government documents. In addition, college libraries give you access to various scholarly journals.

You should also make use of the librarians themselves. Many students are hesitant to seek help from the librarians, but part of a librarian's job is, precisely, to assist you in your information search.

Sometimes you can go directly to an expert and conduct an **interview**. If you intend to interview someone, make certain that they have the proper credentials and expertise. Just because your good friend once had an experience related to your speech topic does not automatically mean they qualify as a solid interview source. At best, you might want to supplement more established research sources with these kinds of data.

Before conducting an interview, you want to have a list of questions ready. The best way to determine these is to first do other research on the topic. That way, you know what information is missing and can try to have the interviewee provide that. It's also simply polite to be prepared; anyone granting an interview is agreeing to devote valuable time to you, so act professionally. It's also wise to have your professor or instructor review your interview questions prior to your conducting the interview.

In this computer age, it's also becoming increasingly popular, if not necessary, to conduct research on the "internet." That term is a bit misleading. The internet is actually a collection of services, one of which is the **world wide web, or WWW**. Most likely, if you're instructed to do "internet research," you're simply being asked to research the WWW.

To research the WWW, you need to go to a search engine. Several popular search engines include Google.com, Lycos.com, Dogpile.com, AltaVista.com, and Ask.com. Simply enter the **URL** (Uniform Resource Locator; in simple terms, the "web address"), type in your keywords, and it will bring up a list of web pages for you.

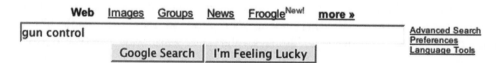

There are at least two concerns to consider when using the WWW. First, you have to determine the proper **keywords**. Sometimes, this can be tricky. For instance, if you type in "gun control," you're likely to find literally thousands of web sites devoted to the topic. You may need to make your keyword search more specific, such as "gun control in Nevada."

Second, the WWW is not well supervised. Anyone can make a web page with information, but that doesn't mean the information is reliable. Indeed, people with agendas are more than happy to create web pages that look very legitimate but that contain blatantly false information.

Certainly, there are a number of legitimate, established organizations with web pages that have nothing to hide. Many newspapers and magazines now have web pages. (See the Appendix for information on how to find newspapers and use the Las Vegas Review Journal online.) Other organizations, such as the Red Cross, are publicly known and undergo scrutiny; they have reputations to maintain and can't afford to provide incorrect information.

If you're uncertain about the legitimacy of a web page you visit, you can at least look for certain key elements. First, can you identify who wrote the information? "Unknown authors" may have something to hide. Second, who is hosting the website? Is it a well-known, legitimate host? Usually, it's best to stick with brand names.

Finally, the website should be more than willing to provide you with its sources of information. If it's legitimate, it will be willing to tell you how it found its data. Ideally, the web site should provide you with links to some of these sources. *If you go to a web site that does not provide you with its sources of information, treat is as suspect and leave it*.

For college students doing work in a college course – such as this one – an ideal alternative is to work with online databases. An **online database** is different from a WWW site in that you have to subscribe to online databases in order to get access to the information. Fortunately for you, CCSN does this subscribing for you.

The important thing about online databases is that they provide access to scholarly research that isn't always available on the WWW. **Scholarly research** is conducted, usually, by people in academic institutions. Its objective is to follow a rigorous process (often scientific), and the research undergoes critical review by experts in the field. Such research is often published in what are called "refereed" or "peer reviewed" journals because the research is evaluated by experts. It is often considered one of the most highly reliable types of information.

These journals are published by nearly every academic discipline and are also sometimes referred to as **scholarly journals**. Many go by the title of "The Journal of . . ." In the Communication field, for example, there are numerous journals, including "The Journal of Communication," "Communication Theory," "Critical Studies in Media Communication," "Quarterly Journal of Speech," etc. If you've chosen an emphasis for your college degree, you can ask your professors to help you identify the primary journals in your field.

You may find it a bit more challenging to work with this material, but you should begin to become more familiar with this kind of research at a college level. Often, you'll find a common structure to such research. For instance, one common structure is to begin the article with a discussion of the problem being researched. That's followed by a discussion about theories or other prior research and what's been learned to date. Next, there will be a proposal (often called the "Methodology" section of the article) for how to address the problem that was discussed. After that, there will be a "Results" section that shows all kinds of scary-looking numbers, charts, and symbols. You'll probably need a research course to fully understand what all of it is saying, but practice reading through this section anyway.

Finally, the article will end with a "Discussion and Conclusion" section, followed by a bibliography. The "Discussion and Conclusion" section tries to explain the results in less technical terms.

Some useful online databases to which you might turn include WebPac, the CQ Researcher, EBSCOhost, and Expanded Academic ASAP. The next chapter will give you specific to utilize the valuable CCSN Library resources.

Citing Your Sources*

When you write a research paper, you're expected to cite the sources you used, both in the paper and in a bibliography. Similarly, when giving a presentation in this class, you're required to cite your sources while speaking and in a bibliography that accompanies your outline.

Any time you obtain ideas and information from someone else, you should give that person, group, organization, or publication its due credit. This is called "**giving attribution**" (or "**citing**" your sources).

Citing sources is required for several reasons. First, it's a courtesy to your audience. It provides them with useful information about where they can learn more about your topic. Second, it also helps you build credibility with your audience. If you've done your research, you will sound like someone who is well educated. The audiences acknowledges that you've sought useful sources of information and that you appear to be current with your topic.

Third, you need to cite sources as a matter of ethics and law. If you acquire information from some source and you pass that information along, then you have to acknowledge where you obtained that information. If you don't do so, it will appear as if you're the person with whom that information originated. At that point, you're taking credit for work that is not yours.

Plagiarism occurs when you present someone else's ideas or information without making it clear that you obtained these from someone else (hence, making it appear as if the work is your own). That is to say, you fail to give proper attribution.

It does not matter whether you're aware of the rules of plagiarism; you're expected to abide by them. If you fail to do so, you'll be subject to various penalties. Penalties for plagiarism can vary from receiving an "F" for the assignment to receiving an "F" for the course (or, in more extreme cases, being expelled from a college).

Students often mistakenly plagiarize in both speeches and papers (or other projects involving "research"). Be careful not to make any of the following common mistakes:

- You can plagiarize if you use a direct, word-for-word quotation and never indicate the source of that quote. In a speech, you should state to your audience that you are quoting directly. In a paper, either use quotation marks or a block paragraph and include the proper attribution.

- You can plagiarize even if you modify a direct, word-for-word quotation and never indicate the source of that near-quote. For instance, a student once indicated that he'd learned a rule that says if you simply change about every 6th word in a quote, it is not plagiarism. That's absolutely false. Either use a direct, word-for-word quote (with proper attribution), or paraphrase the quote (that is, restate it in your own words - but still give attribution; see below).

- You can plagiarize by presenting your own ideas and conclusions (or "points" you wish to make) and failing to identify the source(s) that inspired your ideas and conclusions. You would not have reached these ideas and conclusions without having read through various sources of information; hence, give credit where it is due. For instance, perhaps you're claiming, "gun control will reduce school violence." If you use a statistic to back that up, identify the source of that statistic. In a speech, this will mean you frequently say something like "according to . . ." In a paper, you typically identify your source immediately after providing the information you obtained from that source.

- You can plagiarize by copying any or all of the work of a fellow student.

- You can plagiarize if nearly half (or more) of your speech or paper consists of direct quotes (or even moderately paraphrased quotes). Instructors or professors who assign research projects expect that the majority of the project will be you expressing what you've learned in your words. If you use too many quotes, it begins to raise the question: Who, actually, wrote your speech or paper? You may be crafty at stringing together other people's words, but what do *you* have to say?

You should always check with your instructor or professor to see if he/she requires a particular style book (MLA and APA are the most common). Refer to the rules in these stylebooks always; this is your best bet for avoiding plagiarism problems. These are discussed in the section on "Citing Sources in Bibliographies" later in this chapter.

In addition, check to see if the campus of your choice has a Writing Center or Communication Lab. There may be a small fee involved, but they can help you with concerns about plagiarism, writing problems, etc. They can check your work or provide other useful information that can help you before you turn in your assignments.

Citing Sources During the Speech

As you speak, you need to cite your sources whenever you provide information that you obtained through your research. You won't need to provide as much information as you do in the bibliography, but there are certain key pieces of information you need to provide.

Whenever you introduce a new source for your information, you should provide their name, the name of the publication, and the year. State it conversationally. For example, you might say, "In a November Newsweek article, Dr. Bob Jones of Harvard University said that 80% of all people who pass public speaking courses go on to become millionaires." If you can't find a name for your source, cite the publication, such as "According to a November Newsweek article on public speaking, 80% of all people who pass public speaking courses go on to become millionaires."

Typically, state the name of your source at the beginning of a sentence rather than at the end. This is how we speak conversationally. If you were having lunch with a friend, you wouldn't say, "We're having an exam next week, Professor Jones told me." No, you would say, "hey, Professor Jones told me we're having an exam next week."

Similarly, in a speech, you wouldn't say, "80% of all people who pass public speaking courses go on to become millionaires, according to Dr. Jones." You'd say, "According to Dr. Jones . . ."

An exception to the foregoing would be when you want to put a little variety into the delivery. Once in awhile, you might use two sentences, giving the attribution in the second sentence, such as saying "80% of all people who pass public speaking courses go on to become millionaires. That's according to Dr. Jones."

If you use the same source more than once, you don't need to repeat all of the information from the first citation. You could, for instance, say something as simple as, "Now, Dr. Jones also tells us that . . ."

If appropriate, you should also try to provide some credentials for your sources as soon as possible. For example, you might say, "According to Dr. Jones - a leading researcher in public speaking from Harvard University - 80% of all people who pass public speaking courses go on to become millionaires."

Be careful, however, not to say something that's too generic. For instance, avoid saying things like "studies show," or "research shows." Instead, tell your audience where you found the information about those studies or that research, such as "According to a June 2000 article in Newsweek, research shows that . . ."

Citing Sources in the Bibliography

In this class, researching a speech is no different than researching a term paper. Both are scholarly activities, and both will, therefore, require a bibliography. A **bibliography** is an alphabetical list of the sources you used. It follows a set of rules that specify how to present the information.

The rules are set by various organizations, particularly the Modern Languages Association (MLA), the American Psychological Association (APA), and Turabian. Here, we'll briefly explore the MLA style then APA.

Modern Languages Association (MLA)

First, you'll need to obtain the MLA rules. There are several sources available, but one created by the CCSN Library is particularly helpful. You can find it online, or there are often free handouts available at the computer labs.

Using MLA is a simple matter of identifying the type of source you have (book, journal article, WWW site, interview, etc.) and following the rules for how to provide that entry. In general, you'll need to double-space and use hanging indents. A **hanging indent** is the opposite of the standard indent you use in a term paper:

Standard indent. Standard indent. Standard indent. Standard indent. Standard indent. Standard indent. Standard indent. Standard indent. Standard indent.

Hanging indent. Hanging indent. Hanging indent. Hanging indent. Hanging indent. Hanging indent. Hanging indent. Hanging indent. Hanging indent.

As an example, suppose you want to list a book in your Works Cited page. Here is the MLA rule for citing a book:

Books— One author

On the Works Cited page, give the author's name, the book's title <u>underlined</u>, the city of publication, a colon, the publisher, and the year of publication.

Andrews, John. <u>Mysteries of the Old West</u>. Boston: Houghton Mifflin, 2004.

Also, you won't actually title your bibliography, "bibliography." Instead, you'll use the term, "**Works Cited**." (In APA style, you use "References.") Here's a sample of a Works Cited page:

Sample Works Cited Page

This list should be alphabetized by the authors' last names (or first word in the title if no author is available). Each source you cite in your essay must appear in the works cited list. This list is used to help a reader locate your sources. Double-space after the heading. The second line of each entry is indented one-half inch, and all references are double-spaced.

Works Cited

Bannon, Jonathan. "Return of the Boys." <u>Contemporary Literary Times</u>. Ed. Gene D.C. Stines and Danny R. Molsen. Vol. 3 Detroit: Galish, 1982. 250-261.

"Constance Miloszc." <u>Contemporary Communication</u>. Ed. Madison Stine and Savannah G. Marowski. Vol. 31. New York: Feed the Meter, 1995. 258-259.

<u>Facts about Fluoride: Fluorides and Fluoridation</u>. American Dental Association. 10 Feb. 1997 <http://www.ada.org/consumer/fluoride/articles/fa01.html>.

American Psychological Association (APA)

Below is a list of sample sources cited in APA style. Note the differences depending on what type of source you are using:

Reference: Single-Author Book

Bleier, L. (1986). <u>Women, feminism and biology: The feminist challenge</u>. New York: Methuen.

Reference: Book with More than One Author

Messer, E., & Chance, R. (1991). <u>Geology of the Indian Ocean</u>. Hartford, CT: University of Hartford Press.

Hesen, J., Carpenter, K., Moriber, H., & Milsop, A. (1983). <u>Computers in the business world</u>. Hartford, CT: Capital Press.

Reference: Book Without Author or Editor Listed

<u>The American Heritage Dictionary (4ᵗʰ ed.)</u>. (2000). Boston: Houghton-Mifflin.

Reference: Journals/Periodicals

Use inclusive page numbers. Do not use the abbreviations "p." or "pp."

Campbell, K. (1998). What really distinguishes and/or ought to distinguish feminist sscholarship in communication studies. <u>Women's Studies in Communication,11</u>, 4-5.

Maddux, K. (1997, March). True stories of the internet patrol. <u>NetGuide Magazine</u>, 88-92.

Reference: Brochure or Pamphlet

The Writing Center of Capital Community-Technical College. (1997).<u>Writing: the goal is variety (4th ed.)</u> [Brochure]. Hartford, CT: Author.

Treat pamphlets created by corporate authors in the same way you would treat an entire book written by a corporate author. Don't forget to identify your resource as [Brochure] or [Pamphlet] within brackets.

Reference: Newspaper Articles

If the article is "signed" (that is, you know the author's name), begin with that author's name. (Notice the discontinuous pages.)

Poirot, C. (1998, March 17). HIV prevention pill goes beyond 'morning after'. <u>The Hartford Courant</u>, pp. F1, F6.

If the author's name is not available, begin the reference with the headline or title in the author position.

Adventures in Las Vegas. (1999, March 15). <u>The Los Angeles Times</u>, E-10.

Reference: Nonprint Media

(film):
Reiner, R (Director). (1980). <u>When Harry met Sally</u> [Film]. MGM.

(film of limited circulation):
Holdt, D. (Producer), & Ehlers, E. (Director). (1997). <u>River at High Summer: The St. Lawrence</u> [Film]. (Available from Merganser Films, Inc., 61 Woodland Street, Room 134, Hartford, CT 06105)

(Cassette):
Lake, F. L. (Author and speaker). (1989). <u>Bias and organizational decision making</u> [Cassette]. Gainesville: Edwards.

(Musical recording):
 DiFranco, A. (2001). Ain't that the way. Reckoning and Revelling [CD]. Buffalo, NY: Righteous Babe Records

Reference: Personal Interview, Phone Conversation
(Interview):
(E. McCade, personal communication, March 28, 2001. Ph. 702.555-1313)

Online article
Klein, Donald F. (1997). Control group in Pharmacoptherapy and psychotherapy evaluations. Treatment, I. Retrieved November 16, 1997 from the World Wide Web: http://www.apa.org/treatment/vol1/97_a1.html

On-line journal, subscriber-based
CRT News. (2001. June 7, 2001). Health care communication [3 paragraphs]. Communication Research and Theory Network [On-line serial]. Available Doc. Number 6063

For more assistance with A.P.A. or M.L.A. see the web pages listed below. Be sure to ask your instructor which format they prefer.

MLA
http://www.ccsn.nevada.edu/library/mla.htm
http://www.lib.usm.edu/~instruct/guides/mla.html

APA
http://www.lib.usm.edu/~instruct/guides/apa.html
http://owl.english.purdue.edu/handouts/research/r_apa.html

Notice that you list your sources in alphabetical order. If you know the author's name, you use their last name for alphabetizing. If there's more than one author, you use the last name of the first author listed for the publication. If there's no known author, you use the title of the article.

Annotated Bibliography

After completing your research and selecting good, credible sources of supporting material it is a good idea to construct your bibliography immediately. By doing so you reduce the risk of losing important citation material and eliminate the headache of trying to answer the question "where did I see that statistic?" A great way to further organize your information is to create an annotated bibliography. Your instructor may or may not require this.

An annotated bibliography will have the same basic layout as a Reference or Works Cited page. The main difference is that after each reference listing you add commentary to the references, telling your reader the particular virtues (or, if necessary, the shortcomings) of that resource. Commentaries should be concise, economical summaries written in sentence fragments. The commentary should begin on a new line, indented slightly from the preceding line. An annotated bibliography can be extremely useful for personal use regarding speech construction because it requires that you are familiar with each resource source you have selected. By organizing your material in this manner you not only help your instructor see where you are going, you help yourself by deciding what claim each source can support.

<u>A.P.A. example:</u>
Katal, P. (1993, August 30). Looking out for their own skin. <u>Newsweek</u>, 43.

Documents the difference in living styles between the Haitian peasant class and Haitian elites; provides specific examples regarding diet where poor Haitians starve and rich Haitians adopt weight loss plans. This article was useful for showing the disparity between rich and poor in Haitian culture. I am considering using this as background in my first point or as an attention device.

* The section on plagiarism was written with assistance by Loretta Fearonce of the CCSN Writing Center.

EXERCISES

1) **Topic Selection Exercise**

   Either have your instructor assign you a topic, or select a topic as a group. Then, using the tree diagramming method, break that topic down into 8 levels.

2) **Research Database Exercise**

   Your instructor will provide you with a list of articles that can be found in some of the databases identified here and described in the Appendix. You are to find those articles online and e-mail them to your instructor, using the e-mail options provided with the articles.

3) **Works Cited Exercise**

   For this exercise, you need to obtain the list of MLA citation rules. (Either get one from the computer lab, or print it from the online CCSN link.) Your instructor will provide you with a list of scrambled bibliographic information. Using your MLA rules, write an appropriate Works Cited page.

7 *Organization and Outlining*

See Pg. 68

Terms to Know

- Outline
- Outline structures
- Claim
- Evidence
- Claim-Evidence link
- Sub-claims
- Coordinating conjunctions
- Repetition
- Priming
- Long-term memory
- Short-term memory
- Verbal road map
- Preview claims
- State facts, not topics
- Repeat claims often
- Repeat claims exactly
- Review claims
- Outlining
- Levels of development
- Tree diagramming
- Coordinate
- Subordinate
- Notation system
- Speech body
- Sign posts
- Internal summaries/previews
- Transition to the conclusion
- Speech introduction
- Attention device
- Audience address

Effective speakers always create outlines to guide them in the presentation process. An **outline** is a method of structuring information according to a set of rules and thinking patterns. As you'll see in this chapter, it's necessary to impose some kind of structure on the evidence and materials you gather for your speech. You can have the greatest evidence in the world, and the strongest claims, but if you don't present these in a form that makes sense, all of your information is pretty much useless.

At the same time, merely imposing a structure does not automatically mean that what you've organized makes total sense. For instance, you can certainly build a house according to proper structural specifications, but if you use shoddy materials, you still have a shoddy house. Similarly, you could structure an argument that says "Tim's shirt is blue, his pants are black, and his shoes have laces. Therefore, he should give me his car." That has proper structure, but the logic behind it is absurd. You simply can't build that kind of claim out of that kind of evidence.

Be aware that different types of information and different types of speech purposes each require specific types of **outline structures**. An outline structure is a particular set of procedures needed to present information in an optimum fashion. For example, information that is geographical in nature may require what's called a spatial structure. Certain types of persuasive arguments may need to follow a motivated sequence.

You'll want to learn more about specific types of outline structures because—frustrating as this may seem at first—there can sometimes be more than one way to organize information. Here you'll find that outlining seems easy in principle but can be quite challenging in practice, particularly if you're looking for the "correct" way to organize information. For instance, consider at least three ways in which the same information could be organized properly:

I. Pets come in four major types and have two major benefits.	I. All four of the major types of pets share the same two benefits.	I. The two major benefits of pets can be experienced regardless of which of the four types of pets you choose.

A. Pets come in four major types
  1. Dogs
  2. Cats
  3. Birds
  4. Fish
B. Pets have two major benefits
  1. Friendship
  2. Health
	A. Dogs
	  1. Friendship benefit
	  2. Health benefit
	B. Cats
	  1. Friendship benefit
	  2. Health benefit
	C. Birds
	  1. Friendship benefit
	  2. Health benefit
	D. Fish
	  1. Friendship benefit
	  2. Health benefit
		A. Friendship
		  1. Dogs
		  2. Cats
		  3. Birds
		  4. Fish
		B. Health
		  1. Dogs
		  2. Cats
		  3. Birds
		  4. Fish

Any of these forms of organization could be "correct," depending upon what you want to accomplish.

Still, there are some types of information that lend themselves to specific types of organization. If you read through the chapters on Informative Speaking and Persuasive Speaking, you'll learn about some specific types of outline structures that are well-suited to particular types of speeches (e.g., spatial structure, motivated sequence, etc.). You'll find that all of them pretty much still rely on the more general claim-evidence structure that will be explored in this chapter. Each of those other chapters, however, provides additional guidelines for how to best organize specific types of information to accomplish specific purposes.

The Claim-Evidence Link

The starting point of any outline is the link between claims and evidence. A fundamental objective of a speech is to produce claims. A **claim** is a statement that you want your audience to understand, think about, and act upon. In much less formal language, it's one of the points you want your audience to get.

Most audiences will not leave your speech remembering a lot of what you had to say. The question is, with what information *will* they leave? Unless you structure your presentation properly, it's quite possible the audience will not leave your speech with the same ideas you want them to have. You must, therefore, produce claims (or your "main points") in order to provide the audience with the ideas you want them to have.

Claims are always linked to evidence or details. (Usually, you have "evidence" in a persuasive speech and "details" in an informative speech. Terms may vary. In this chapter, we'll refer to it simply as "evidence.") **Evidence** is information you gather (through research) to support or clarify a claim. It can take the form of statistics, testimony, examples, principles, or emotional appeals. (See the chapter on Research for specific information about these.)

Once you've gathered your evidence together, you use various thinking processes to extract claims from it. (See the chapters on Persuasion & Reasoning and Informative Speaking for specific information about this.) Visually, the **claim-evidence link** will look like this:

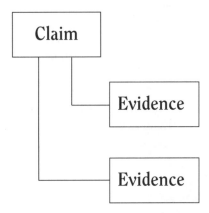

In an outline, the claim-evidence link might look something like this:

A. Claim: Gun control will save lives
      1. Evidence: FBI statistics from 2002 show that states with gun control had 25% fewer gun deaths.
      2. Evidence: A leading expert from the Anti-Gun Coalition claims that it just makes common sense to regulate gun ownership.

Sometimes a speaker attempts to express several ideas at once. **Sub-claims** arise when a claim expresses two or more related ideas. For instance, you might want to make the argument that "the death penalty is immoral and illegal." (It is in some states.) Here, you're actually making two claims at once: the death penalty is immoral, and the death penalty is illegal.

One way to determine if you have sub-claims is to look for **coordinating conjunctions**, which are words such as: **and, or, but, however, thus, therefore, etc.** These words indicate that you're connecting two or more independent clauses, or units of thought. Look at the following example:

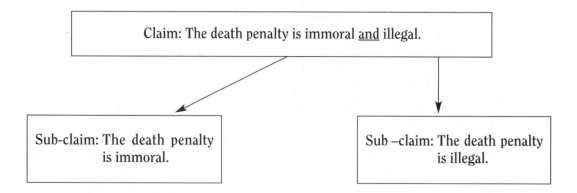

An outline of this structure would look as follows:

A. Claim: The death penalty is immoral and illegal.
    1. Sub-claim: The death penalty is immoral
        a. Evidence
        b. Evidence
    2. Sub-claim: The death penalty is illegal
        a. Evidence
        b. Evidence

If using sub-claims, be certain the ideas are actually related to each other. For instance, it probably makes sense to say "Yoga builds strength and flexibility," but you'd be pushing the wrong agenda to say "Yoga builds strength, and NATO should be disbanded."

Guidelines for Organizing and Presenting Claims

Now that you know the basic unit of an outline—the claim-evidence link—it's important to recognize some conditions that govern their use in an outline. In particular, you'll discover that outlines (and the presentations that come from them) involve a lot of **repetition** of main ideas. Sometimes this repetition seems annoying, but there are good reasons why it must be present in a speech.

First, audiences are engaged in a listening activity. In real life, this means that while you're speaking, people will be coughing, sneezing, talking, answering cell phones, squirming, getting up to leave, coming in late, pondering the fight they just had with their significant other, worrying about the project that's overdue . . . you name it. Many factors can get in the way between your ideas and your audience's ability to simply hear them, much less understand them.

As such, you have to make extra efforts to ensure that your points are heard and understood in the way you want them to be heard and understood. In a sense, you have to do some of the thinking for the audience, and outlining provides this means of thinking. Many of the principles of outlining discussed in this chapter come from our knowledge of audiences and their thinking processes via research done in the fields of rhetoric, psychology, and education.

Think of it this way. If you were trying to get news from a newspaper, you'd have total control over that information. You can pick it up, read it, think about it, put it down, come back to it later, etc. On the other hand, if you obtained your news from a radio newscast, then if you sneeze in the middle of the story, you've missed the story and have to wait for it to be repeated.

Similarly, audiences can quickly miss what you have to say if they're not paying proper attention at a given moment.

In addition, it's useful to recognize that audiences need to be primed to hear certain ideas. **Priming** is a concept from psychology that says we are better able to receive information if we're first prepared for it. For instance, if you were going to talk about dogs, you would be better to first say "I'm going to talk about dogs." By doing so, the audience can begin recalling what it knows about dogs. It can then better link your new information with what they already know, and learning can be more effective.

Remember, also, that people have memory limits. We have two basic kinds of memory. **Long-term memory** is the concepts and experiences we have to make sense of information we encounter. **Short-term memory** refers to the temporary storage system we use for any new, incoming information. As your audience hears you, the words go into their short-term memories, and then only some of that information will make its way into their long-term memories. Indeed, short-term memory can handle only about 7 new pieces of information at any given time.

Even in a short speech, then, the audience will be lucky to remember maybe 2-3 things you actually had to say. The question is, *which* 2-3 things will they remember? Chances are, you want them to remember you claims, and you want them to understand your claims in a particular way. (It would be disastrous, for example, for an audience member to walk away from a speech on CPR thinking, "let's see . . . first I break the ribs . . . ").

Based on this understanding of audience perceptions and limits, certain rules have evolved over time to govern how outlines should be structured in order to counter-act some of these limitations. An old rule of outlining was "tell them what you're going to do, do it, and tell them what you've done." Here, we can modify that a bit by saying "tell them what they're going to learn, teach them, and tell them what they've learned."

This way of thinking is consistent with general rules of outlining and with the way thinking takes place generally. Outlines serve at least two primary purposes. First, they help you, the speaker, develop and organize your thinking. Second, they help you provide your audience with a **verbal road map** of your speech. That is to say, your speech will constantly be telling your audience where you have been and where you intend to go next in the development of your ideas. You have to lead your audience through the speech without being patronizing about it.

If an audience doesn't have a copy of your speech in front of them, they're forced to follow your information exclusively through a listening process. If you present information to them in specific ways to help them anticipate and follow your words, you make it easier for them to understand and respond to your facts and ideas. In this regard, following these guidelines for claims when developing your outline:

• *Preview claims*

Always open with your claims; never lead up to them. There are certainly speeches where it's appropriate to be suspenseful and lead to a point. In most speeches, however, this approach can work against you. It's typically better to "spoil the surprise" and simply tell them up front exactly what you intend to say.

Suppose, for example, that you were once again giving a speech on gun control. Imagine a speaker saying the following:

"We've had too many school shootings. In fact, random violence is greater than ever, and illegal gun sales are on the rise. Clearly, we need gun control."

The speaker's claim that we need gun control seems to follow from that kind of evidence, but think first about the mental processes the audience will go through before hearing this claim. The first thing they've heard is "we've had too many school shootings." That doesn't automatically mean we need control, and neither will the notion of gun control automatically come to mind. Perhaps, instead, an audience member might be thinking "this means we need more school safety." Similarly, an audience member might think that "random violence is greater than ever" means a lapse in social moral values, not necessarily a need for gun control.

In other words, if you give your evidence first, there are too many interpretations that can be made for that evidence. By the time you actually get to your claim, you audience members may each have reached a very different conclusion about what all of the evidence means. Then, when they finally hear your claim, they have to mentally scramble and try to remember everything you just said to see if it makes sense in terms of your claim. While they're doing that, you're already talking about your next claim, and everybody is now behind, and you have nothing but a mess.

On the other hand, if you open with the claim, "we need gun control," now the audience has a context by which to make sense of the evidence that will follow. They can ask themselves, "well, do too many school shootings necessarily mean the need for gun control?" Note that while they might not agree with your claim, at least you and the audience are on the same page about the point you're trying to make.

This method of giving the claim ahead of time is called **previewing** your claim. As you'll see when we examine the various parts of a speech, you'll be previewing your major claims in the speech introduction.

• *State facts, not topics*

As noted, your audience will remember only a few things you say in a presentation. As such, you want to try to ensure that the audience remembers very specific facts. To do so, you have to **state facts, not topics**. That is to say, don't just tell them what you'll talk about; tell them specifically what they'll learn. Note the difference in the following example:

Stating the topic: Next, I'll talk about the history of the computer.
Stating the fact: Next, you'll learn that the computer's history actually dates back over 2000 years, beginning with the development of a crude adding machine.

• *Repeat claims often*

Not only should you preview specific claims, you should also repeat claims often. Again, when you see the full outline format later in this chapter, you'll discover that your primary claims—those facts and ideas you want the audience to understand, remember, and act upon—will be stated at least once in each of the three parts of the speech (the introduction, body, and conclusion). Here again, this repetition is necessary because of the limits of audience perceptions and memories.

• *Repeat claims exactly*

In English composition courses, you're often told to avoid being repetitive and to vary your wording in creative ways. This is not so in a presentation. English composition is intended for an audience that reads, whereas speeches are intended for an audience that listens. Reading and listening involve very different types of mental activity and even engage different portions of the brain. As such, you have to apply different rules when giving speeches.

If you vary the wording of your claims in a speech, then there's a good possibility that the audience will begin to get confused as to exactly what point you're trying to make. By repeating claims as exactly as possible in all three parts of the speech, you enhance the audience's opportunities to hear and comprehend your points.

• *Review claims*

By now, you've learned that the audience will hear your claims in all three parts of the speech, including the conclusion. In the conclusion, you're giving your audience a reminder of what they learned that day as well as giving them one last chance to fully grasp that these are the facts and idea they are supposed to remember.

Developing Levels of Facts and Ideas

Now that you understand the nature of claims and their links to evidence, you're ready to being outlining. Just to be realistic, **outlining** is the time-consuming process of organizing thoughts according to the rules of structuring information. The emphasis here is on "time-consuming." You can't do this the night before the speech is due without a lot of stress.

For this class, you're not going to be writing manuscripts, but you will write full-sentence outlines (as well as bibliographies; see the Research chapter). This means, first, that you need to break your facts and ideas down into **levels of development**. That is to say, you have to break facts and ideas into smaller "parts."

It may be easiest to simply illustrate this concept visually. You might also refer to the chapter on Research as part of this discussion. Let's say you're writing a speech about the media. That's a very broad topic, so you might want to break it down into smaller sub-topics, perhaps as follows:

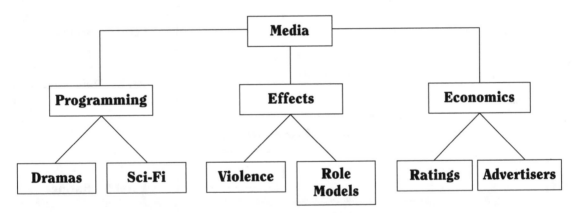

This method of working with information is called **tree diagramming**, because it "branches out" at new levels of related ideas. Notice that information keeps being broken down, or branched, into new levels:

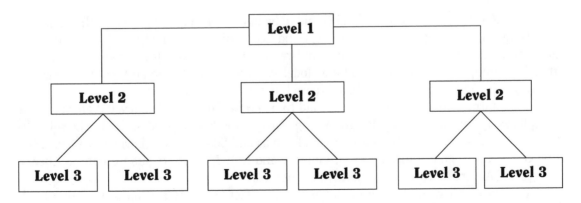

We could, of course, break each level down into further levels. Level 4, for instance, would have more specific information about different kinds of dramas (Soap Operas, Police Shows, Medical Shows, etc.). You could choose the topic of your speech at any of these levels and then break it down further still.

We can also look at this same organization by presenting it sideways. Once you do so, you begin to see the kind of logic followed in creating outlines:

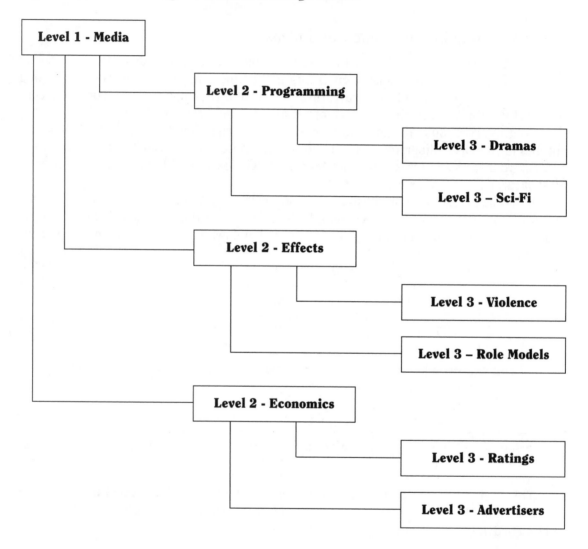

Any information on the same level is said to be **coordinate** information. In this example, everything at Level 2—Programming, Effects, and Economics—are said to be at coordinate levels to each other. Similarly, the groupings of Dramas and Sci-Fi shows are coordinate to each other. The groupings of Violence and Role Models are coordinate to each other. The groupings of Ratings and Advertisers are coordinate to each other.

Any information at a deeper level is said to be **subordinate** to the level(s) above it. For example, everything at Level 2—Programming, Effects, and Economics—is said to be subordinate to Level 1—Media. Also in our example, Dramas and Sci-Fi shows (Level 3) are said to be subordinate to Programming (Level 2). Violence and Role Models are subordinate to Effects. Ratings and Advertisers are subordinate to Economics.

If you notice, in all of these examples, whenever a fact or idea is developed at another level, there are at least two facts or ideas at the new level. In other words, wherever there's an "A," there's also at least a "B." Wherever there's a "1," there's also at least a "2." And so on. **When-**

ever you move to a new level of development, always have at least 2 facts or ideas in that new level. You would, thus, want to avoid the following kind of outline structure:

```
II. Body
    A. Claim 1
        1. Evidence
    B. Claim2
        1. Evidence
        2. Evidence
```

Again, you have to follow proper methods of logic and thinking as part of this process of breaking facts and ideas into levels. Just because something follows a structure doesn't mean it's necessarily logical. Refer, again, to the chapters on Research, Persuasion & Reasoning, and Informative Speaking to better understand the thought processes behind the development of facts and ideas.

Using Notation Systems

If you understand the idea of breaking facts and ideas into levels, then it's no more difficult to begin to assign numbers and letters to these levels. The following illustration shows this relationship, both with and without the "Levels" labels.

Level 1 - Media	**I. Media**
Level 2 - Programming	**A. Programming**
Level 3 - Dramas	**1. Dramas**
Level 3 - Sci-Fi	**2. Sci-Fi**
Level 2 - Effects	**B. Effects**
Level 3 - Violence	**1. Violence**
Level 3 - Role Models	**2. Role Models**
Level 2 - Economics	**C. Economics**
Level 3 - Ratings	**1. Ratings**
Level 3 - Advertisers	**2. Advertisers**

To determine how to number and letter these different levels, you have to rely upon a **notation system**, which is the process of assigning numbers and letters to facts and ideas according to a set of rules. The typical rule is to alternate between numbers and letters each time you move to a deeper level. In general, you'll follow this kind of sequence. Note that each time you move in a level, you also indent:

  I.
      A.
          1.
              a.
                  (1)
                      (a)
                          1
                              a

If we apply this to a simple example, it might look as follows.

I. Pets come in many varieties.
  A. A dog is a type of pet.
    1. Dogs serve many functions in the household.
      a. One function is to be a watchdog.
        (1) A watchdog protects your home.

For most speeches, you won't develop ideas much beyond the fifth level. Be aware that where you start applying the numbers and letters may vary with your professor's or instructor's requirements. For example, both of the following short outlines use legitimate notation systems:

Introduction	**I. Introduction**
I. Attention Device	**A. Attention Device**
II. Thesis statement	**B. Thesis statement**
III. Claims	**C. Claims**
A. Claim 1	**1. Claim 1**
B. Claim 2	**2. Claim 2**
Body	**II. Body**
I. Claim 1	**A. Claim 1**
A. Evidence	**1. Evidence**
B. Evidence	**2. Evidence**
II. Claim 2	**B. Claim 2**
A. Evidence	**1. Evidence**
B. Evidence	**2. Evidence**
Conclusion	**III. Conclusion**
I. Restate thesis	**A. Restate thesis**
II. Restate claims	**B. Restate claims**
A. Claim 1	**1. Claim 1**
B. Claim 2	**2. Claim 2**
III. Memorable statement	**C. Memorable statement**

The Speech Body

Now that you understand the basic units and concepts of outlining, you're ready to actually begin outlining the speech. Here, you want to begin with the speech body. Why start there and not with the introduction? Well, first, the **speech body** *is* the speech. It should be the first part of the speech you finalize. Granted, your speech will begin with some kind of introduction. But you can't finalize the introduction until you've developed the speech body properly and actually know what you have to say. As such, if you try to start by writing your introduction first, you'd also better be prepared to revise the introduction frequently.

How much of the speech body you develop depends upon how elaborate you have to be with your information. In general, you can expect to use either of the following two outline forms. (They differ only in their notation systems.)

```
Body                              II. Body
I. Claim 1                            A. Claim 1
   A. Sign Post/Evidence                 1. Sign Post/Evidence
   B. Sign Post/ Evidence                2. Sign Post/Evidence

Internal Summary/Preview          Internal Summary/Preview

II. Claim 2                           B. Claim 2
   A. Sign Post/Evidence                 1. Sign Post/Evidence
   B. Sign Post/ Evidence                2. Sign Post/Evidence

Internal Summary/Preview          Internal Summary/Preview

III. Claim 3                          C. Claim 3
   A. Sign Post/Evidence                 1. Sign Post/Evidence
   B. Sign Post/ Evidence                2. Sign Post/Evidence

Internal Summary                  Internal Summary

Transition to Conclusion          Transition to Conclusion
```

Transition Statements in the Speech Body

We've already discussed claims, evidence, and the claim-evidence link. Two new items you see in the speech body are sign posts and internal summaries/previews. **Sign posts** are words or short phrases that introduce evidence. (They can also be used in other parts of the speech, if appropriate.) Some samples of sign posts include:

- since
- previously
- later
- earlier
- eventually
- in the past
- next
- furthermore
- in addition to

- moreover
- but
- however
- on the other hand
- likewise
- in comparison
- unfortunately
- in spite of
- on the contrary

- therefore
- consequently
- thus
- according to
- so
- due to
- since
- because of
- also

Sign posts can also include "first," "second," "third," etc. An example of a claim-evidence link in the speech body, then, might look as follows:

A. <u>Claim</u>: Gun control because would save lives by lowering the crime rate and protecting children

   1. <u>Sign Post</u>/<u>Evidence</u>: <u>First</u>, a 1999 FBI study claims it would save lives by lowering the crime rate.

   2. <u>Sign Post</u>/<u>Evidence</u>: <u>Also</u>, as NRA statistics prove, it will protect children.

Be careful. We often link terms like "first," "second," etc. with claims. If using these with claims and evidence, be careful to word everything properly. You wouldn't want to say something like "First, gun control would save lives. First, a 1999 FBI study , . . " That would confuse. Instead, try saying something more conversational, such as "the first major point I want to make is that gun control would save lives. Let's consider, first, that a 1999 FBI study claims . . ."

Also, make certain you use sign posts that correspond. For instance, you don't want to start with "on the one hand" if the next piece of evidence doesn't clearly lend itself to "on the other hand." (It would be odd to say "on the one hand" followed by, say, "in addition to that." It would also be odd to use any "hands" if more than two points are involved. Would you say, "on the third hand?")

Just as you attach sign posts to evidence, so should you link **internal summaries/previews** with claims. These are statements that summarize the point you're leaving while also providing transition to the next point you want to make. In a sense, you're simply restating the claim you just left and previewing the next claim.

Internal summaries certainly make the speech seem especially repetitious, but remember, when you're giving speeches that are 15 minutes, 20 minutes, 30 minutes, etc. in length, you increase the chances of the audience getting lost. You need to periodically remind them of what's going on, via the verbal road map concept that was mentioned earlier. Even if you give shorter speeches in this class, it's important to practice these.

For that matter, unlike claims, you probably don't need to state your internal summaries exactly. The goal here is to provide transition in a conversational manner. As such, you might modify the wording a little and allow some creativity at this point.

As an example, take a look at the following:

II. Body

   A. Claim: Gun control reduces school violence

      1. Evidence: First, studies prove this

      2. Evidence: Plus, a legal expert claims this

INTERNAL SUMMARY: As you can see, school violence seems to go down where gun control's been tried. But people still have other worries, particularly when it appears their rights may be jeopardized. As I'd like to show you next, however . . .

   B. Claim: Gun control can still protect Constitutional rights

In this speech body, we see two primary claims: gun control reduces school violence, and it can protect Constitutional rights. In the actual speech, you would first go through your discussion of Claim 1, citing your evidence about gun control and school violence (and being sure to use sign posts).

Once you finish that discussion, you're ready to move on to the second claim. Before doing so, however, stop and remind the audience of what they've just learned. Then begin to lead them smoothly into the next claim.

When using internal summaries, be sure you're clear that you're summarizing. You need to say things like, "so as you just saw," or "before I move on, let me just emphasize, again . . ." If you don't use wording of this kind, it's possible the audience won't realize you're summarizing and may think you're simply elaborating on the last piece of evidence you were discussing.

Note that you should have an internal summary for every claim in the speech body. You need to be sure to include one for the last claim. Obviously, however, you won't have another claim to preview at that point, so you need instead to prepare the audience for your conclusion.

Here, then, you need to provide a **transition to the conclusion**, which is a short statement that simply indicates you're about to wrap things up. This can be something as simple as "in conclusion." For a more personal and professional effect, however, you might want to have a slight bit of pause and then say something like, "okay, I've covered a lot of ideas today. Let me try to wrap all of this up for you now."

The Speech Introduction

It's difficult to say that any one part of a speech is more important than any other. Each serves its functions. Nonetheless, the **speech introduction** plays a particularly critical role, since it's your first contact with the audience and establishes the overall tone of the presentation. We know from research in social psychology that people tend to make judgments of one another within the first 30 seconds of meeting them. What you say and do in the introduction, then, could make a significant difference in how the overall presentation is experienced.

It was noted that the speech body is the first part of the speech you should finalize. The introduction is actually the last part of the speech you should finalize. We're covering the introduction before the conclusion (the second part to finalize) because it introduces some ideas that are useful for better understanding conclusions.

The introduction is your contract with the audience. It indicates to them that they are the center of your attention, and you'll be making a series of promises that you'll be fulfilling in the speech body. In essence, the audience has the right to know what it's getting into; you are, after all, asking them to devote their precious time to what you have to say.

In that regard, the introduction should accomplish several objectives, each of which is achieved by presenting certain kinds of information. Patterns for introductions vary, but two common ones are as follows:

Introduction	**I. Introduction**
I. Attention device: open with impact	**A. Attention device**
II. Link to topic	**B. Audience address**
III. Connect to audience, provide credibility statement	**C. Background material**
	D. Thesis/purpose statement
IV. Thesis statement	**E. Preview claims**
V. Preview (main points)	**F. Transition to body**
VI. Transition to body	

In either model, you begin with some kind of attention device. The attention device is meant to establish immediate interest in the topic. Do NOT open with something weak, such as "today I'm going to talk about . . ." Save that for later.

Instead, use some kind of device. Common devices include:

- Quotation
- Illustration
- Joke or humorous tale
- Question
- Startling statistic or fact
- Short narrative
- Reference to a historical event
- Personal story
- Reference the occasion
- Reference to preceding speeches

There are a few types of attention devices that you want to handle with caution. Sometimes speakers open with a survey, where they want the audience to give a show of hands ("how many of you . . .?"). Audiences might not want to be participatory and put on the spot. Also, what happens if you don't get the show of hands you expected? The very first thing you've done is fall flat on your face.

Similarly, jokes can be quickly offensive to some audience members. Further, what if the joke bombs? Again, you might not want to fall flat on your face.

Once you have their attention, you next want to have audience address. ("Link to topic" and "Connect to audience" provide the same kinds of information.) The idea of **audience address** is to help the audience understand that there's something of value in this presentation for them. Your job as a speaker is to help them understand why they need to hear about this topic. Here, you need to make this personal. Use personal pronouns such as "you," "us," "we," etc.

As an example, suppose you're giving a speech on panic attacks. Certainly, you can relate this topic to your fellow class members rather quickly and personally: "I'm sure all of you in here have experienced some level of anxiety, knowing you'll be giving a speech. Well, I'm here to day to talk to you about panic attacks. They affect not only you but a good number of people from all walks of life."

Having established a need to listen, you might next want to give some **background material** in order to continue building interest and warming the audience up to the subject. The background material is useful for helping the audience see the bigger picture. For instance, you obviously won't have time to discuss all that you learned in your research on the topic. You could, however, identify some of this other information at this point in the speech, noting famous people, events, etc. with which the audience may be familiar. You might also want to spend some time discussing any technical terms or ideas that will be useful to know when you get into the speech body.

Before giving background material, it's helpful to let your audience know that this is what you're doing. (Say, "Before I get started today, let me first give you a little bit of background on this topic.") Also, the background material can be a great place to begin citing sources and introducing your research, since this helps build credibility.

Sometimes speakers also feel the need to provide some **credibility material** about themselves. They provide information which explains why they're qualified to speak on this subject, whether it is their experiences, their education, their research, or all of these. For example, if you were giving a speech on the Philippines and you had lived there for 15 years, sharing this with the audience could boost your credibility.

Once the audience has a good sense of where you're going with all of this, you're ready to introduce your **thesis**, or **purpose statement**. Your thesis is your statement of what you intend to accomplish that day. It tries to provide some main or central point around which your claims will make sense. It's usually equivalent to your purpose for speaking that day. For example, it might be to say "I'm here to today to try to convince you that cats make the best pets," or "I hope today to teach you the three most important points about interpersonal conflict resolution."

For practical purposes, the thesis in a persuasive speech will typically be your stance an issue (e.g., "we need to legalize euthanasia"; see the chapter on Persuasion & Reasoning.) For an informative speech, the thesis will be a summary of the nature of your claims (e.g., "there are 3 steps involved in . . ."; see the chapter on Informative Speaking.)

Next, you need to state your claims, or preview them as was indicated earlier. Be certain you word them as identically as possible with their corresponding claims in the boy and conclusion. Also, be certain they're presented in the same order as in the speech body.

Finally, you're ready to begin the speech (i.e., the body), so you want to provide a brief **transition to the speech body**, which is a simple statement such as "so, let's begin with my first major point, which is that . . ."

The Speech Conclusion

The second part of the speech you should finalize is the conclusion. The **speech conclusion** is the last opportunity the audience has to hear your claims, and it also provides useful direction and motivation for the audience once the speech is finished. It's the last words your audience will hear, and it's the last impression with which you'll leave them, so you don't want to simply end with "I'm done" or "and that's it." Those are considered to be poor form.

In general, the conclusion will have one of the following outline forms (again, the difference being the notation system):

Conclusion	III. Conclusion
I. Restate Purpose/Thesis	**A. Restate Purpose/Thesis**
II. Restate Claims	**B. Restate Claims**
A. Restate Claim 1	**1. Restate Claim 1**
B. Restate Claim 2	**2. Restate Claim 2**
C. Restate Claim 3	**3. Restate Claim 3**
III. Motivate to action/Give useful direction	**C. Motivate to action/Give useful direction**
IV. Close with memorable statement	**D. Close with memorable statement**

First, you'll begin with a restatement of your purpose/thesis. This should be worded nearly identically with that from your speech introduction. Similarly, follow this by restating you claims, again as identically as possible with those in the speech introduction and conclusion.

Next, you want to provide **motivation to action**, wherein you give useful direction and try to reconnect with your audience. Here, you might want to re-emphasize the importance of the topic as well as any attitudes you want the audience to change or adopt. Also, you can identify specific behaviors that can be taken, such as identifying further sources of information to which the audience can turn.

Finally, it's time to end the presentation. Here, you want to leave your audience with some kind of **memorable statement** that will leave them with an impression; make some sort of impact on the audience. You could choose from the various types of devices you used for the attention device:

- Quotation
- Illustration
- Joke or humorous tale
- Question
- Startling statistic or fact

- Short narrative
- Reference to a historical event
- Personal story
- Reference the occasion
- Reference to preceding speeches

It would, however, be bad form to simply use the exact same device with which you opened your presentation. You could, however, close with a similar device (e.g., open with a statistic, close with a different statistic). One other useful method would be to open with part of a story, give the speech, and then close with a conclusion to the opening story.

Using Templates to Write Your Outlines

Outlines are best created using a word processor. Even if you don't own a computer, as a paying CCSN student, you are entitled to use the computer labs and their word processing facilities. You should learn to work with a word processor, not only for this class but simply to be a successful student in general.

Because you'll have to write several outlines for different types of speeches, we've simplified some of the time-consuming process and are providing templates you can use to create your outlines. An outline **template** is simply a document that has all of the "parts" ready to go; you simply fill in the details. That's where your thinking and research will come into play.) The templates are available on the Department of Communication home page. Your professor or instructor can provide more information about how to find and use these.

Overview of Outline Requirements and a Sample Outline

The following is a side-by-side comparison of the general instructions for an outline and an applied example. Please note that the example is a fictitious persuasive speech; you would, obviously, modify the wording for an informative speech. The spacing is also slightly odd, in order to allow the side-by-side comparisons.

I. Introduction

    A. Attention Device (Story, Startling Statistic, Quote, etc.)

I. Introduction

    A. Attention Device: It's been estimated by the American Psychological Association that most of you witnessed over 500,000 murders or other acts of violence by the time you reached age 18. Given the recent spate of shootings throughout the U.S., perhaps we should seriously consider media violence.

B. Audience Address (Why does the audience need to hear this? what's in it for them?)

1. Identify nature & significance of topic

2. Discuss how topic relates to audience's needs & interests (specifically, how does this relate to your actual fellow class-mates?)

C. Background Material (For shorter speeches, such as done in this class, you might emphasize only two of these; be sure to explain to audience that this is back-ground material)

1. Historical developments

2. Vital issues/controversies

3. Important people/events
4. Special terminology
5. Credibility material

D. State Speech Purpose/Thesis (What do you hope to accomplish with this speech? What will the audience learn or be moti-vated to think or do?)

E. State Claims
   1. State Claim 1 (should be consistent with Speech Body and Conclusion)

   2. State Claim 2 (should be consistent with Speech Body and Conclusion)

   3. State Claim 3 (should be consistent with Speech Body and Conclusion)

F. Provide transition to Body

II. Body
   A. Claim 1 (should be consistent with Intro-duction & Conclusion)
      1. Sign Post/Evidence

B. Audience Address:

1. Media violence bombards us all through TV, movies, videos, video games, songs, and comic books.

2. All of us in this room watch TV, listen to music, etc. None of us in here can escape exposure to at least some media violence, so a better understanding of it may liter-ally be a life-saver.

C. Background Material: Before I make that case, let me give you a little background information on this subject.

1. It may surprise you to learn that not every-one thinks media violence is harmful.

2. In fact, a 1996 study by the American Psy-chological Association claims that we really haven't learned anything reliable about the effects of media in the past several decades.

3. But the debate about media violence is a long-standing one; Media scholar Melvin DeFleur has referred to it as the "legacy of fear."

D. Speech Purpose/Thesis: I hope today to convince you that the media do not have the kinds of powers in our lives that we often think they do; we, the audience, are in control.

E. Claims:
   1. Claim 1 One reason why this is so is that we mistakenly think the media affect us directly

   2. Claim 2 You'll also see that media research is biased

   3. Claim 3 Finally, I'll show you that media research is inconsistent.

F. Transition to Body: Let's begin by looking at my first reason, which is that . . .

II. Body
   A. Claim 1: . . . we mistakenly think the media affect us directly
      1. Sign Post/ Evidence 1: First, Anderson & Meyer say all media content must be interpreted (cite book passage)

2. Sign Post/Evidence

2. Sign Post/Evidence 2: <u>For that matter</u>, Schoening says media do not send "messages" (example from his research)

INTERNAL SUMMARY OF CLAIM 1

INTERNAL SUMMARY OF CLAIM 1: It's hard to believe, then, that media have such direct control over us. At the same time, we should also recognize that . . .

B. Claim 2 (should be consistent with Introduction & Conclusion)

B. Claim 2: . . . media research is biased.

1. Sign Post/Evidence

1. Sign Post/ Evidence 1: Consider, <u>first</u> ,that leading scholar Melvin DeFleur's says that all media research serves political purposes (give quote)

2. Sign Post/Evidence

2. Sign Post/Evidence 2: <u>Also</u>, note that Stuart Hall shows us how media research never looks at all sides of an issue (cite Fiske book)

INTERNAL SUMMARY OF CLAIM 2

INTERNAL SUMMARY OF CLAIM 2: I don't think it's any surprise, then, that we're led to believe in the "dangers" of our media, given how one-side that research is. But if that doesn't convince you, consider my final point, which is that . . .

C. Claim 3 (should be consistent with Introduction & Conclusion)

C. Claim 3: . . . media research is inconsistent

1. Sign Post/Evidence

1. Sign Post/ Evidence 1: <u>First</u> , take a look at a recent APA study that shows we've found no conclusive evidence of effects in over 50 years

2. Sign Post/Evidence

2. Sign Post/Evidence 2: <u>Second</u>, consider Shaffer's study on pornography which showed clear conflicts between major research

INTERNAL SUMMARY OF CLAIM 3

INTERNAL SUMMARY OF CLAIM 3: So, we can't even really say with any confidence that our media have any effects on us, much less harmful ones.

TRANSITION TO CONCLUSION (A sentence or two)

TRANSITION TO CONCLUSION: "Okay, then, let me try to wrap all of this up for you."

III. Conclusion

III. Conclusion

A. Purpose/Thesis

A. Restate Purpose/Thesis: Today I tried to prove to you that the media do not directly affect us in powerful ways.

B. Restate Claims

B. Restate Claims:

1. Restate Claim 1 (should be consistent with Speech Introduction and Body)

1. Claim 1: I showed you first that we mistakenly think the media affect us directly

2. **Restate** **Claim** **2** (should be consistent with Speech Introduction and Body)

3. **Restate** **Claim** **3** (should be consistent with Speech Introduction and Body)

C. **Motivate to action/Give useful direction** (For shorter speeches, such as done in this class, you might emphasize only two of these)

1. Emphasize the importance of the issue(s)

2. Identify attitudes to change or adopt

3. Identify specific behaviors that can be taken, or identify further sources of information

D. **Close with memorable statement** (A different Story, Startling Statistic, Quote, etc.)

2. **Claim 2:** Next, I showed you how media research is biased

3. **Claim 3**: Finally, I showed you that media research is inconsistent

C. **Motivate to action/Give useful direction**:

1. Obviously, this issue is complex and won't go away.

2. I encourage you to not just jump on bandwagons to eliminate any kind of media content; the First Amendment is at stake.

3. I highly recommend that you read the book, "Media Literacy: A Social Action Approach" by Anderson & Schoening.

D. **Memorable statement**: Before ending, I'd like to leave you with a quote from Anderson's article: "Media never have effects outside of what goes on in our daily lives. If you want to understand media, you have to look at how people use media on a day-to-day basis."

8 *Presentation Aids*

Terms to Know:

- Presentation aids
- Actual objects
- Models
- Photographs
- Line drawings
- Diagrams
- Maps
- Graphs and charts
- Posters
- Handouts

- Slides (35 mm & computer-based)
- Overhead transparencies
- Video
- Pre-recorded music
- Pre-recorded oration
- Emphasize key points
- Break down complex information
- Learning styles
- Rules for presentation aids

We live in an electronic world where visual and auditory stimuli literally bombard us through TV, movies, radio, CDs, MP3s, etc. We also now live in age where computers, video, DVD, etc. are commonly integrated into presentations. Knowing how to effectively use these devices to enhance your presentations can go a long way toward creating an effective experience for both you and your audience. This chapter will explore various types of visual aids, rules for their use, and rules for their design.

What are Presentation Aids?

Presentation aids are visual or auditory materials that are used to enhance or clarify your speech information. Any number of materials can constitute a presentation aid:

Actual objects are pretty much anything you can fit through the door, although you have to be practical about what you bring to show. For example, one of the rules of visual aids (see the section on rules later in this chapter) says that visuals must be visible to people in the back

Transparency

row. That being the case, you might not want to bring your arrowhead collection as a visual aid, unless you're allowed to pass them around.

For that matter, some objects are just impractical to bring (e.g., a car). In lieu of actual objects, speakers sometimes use **models** of objects instead. For instance, one student once brought a set of plastic lungs that were donated to her by the American Lung Association. The model lungs showed the difference between those of a healthy person and those of a smoker.

Photographs can be fine substitutes when actual objects aren't available. It would certainly be hard to bring the actual Grand Canyon to class, but a photo might do nicely. If you intend to put photos on overhead transparencies, be aware that (for technical reasons) you're likely to lose a lot of visual quality. If you need a photograph to provide fine details, overheads might not be the wisest route.

Sometimes a **line drawing** works better than a photo. Line drawings are useful, for instance, when you need to highlight only specific visual information. They can also minimize the harshness of some images. For instance, students giving speeches about late-term abortion have often used a series of line drawings that depict the procedure; actual photos might be difficult for some audience members to deal with.

Maps, of course, help give an audience a sense of spatial location, distance, and proportion. There are various kinds of maps, such as road maps and topographical maps. Sometimes maps are also used to show various numerical figures, such as death penalty rates in various states.

Graphs and charts are used to provide statistical information and also come in a variety of presentation styles. For instance, you could present the same information in any of the following types of graphs:

Certain kinds of graphs, however, tend to be most common and appropriate to typical kinds of data. For instance, a *pie graph* shows relationships among parts (e.g., the allotments of a budget).

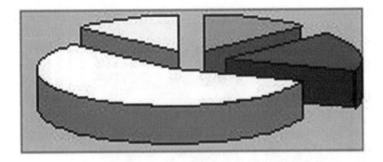

A *bar graph*, on the other hand, is useful for comparing and contrasting items and information.

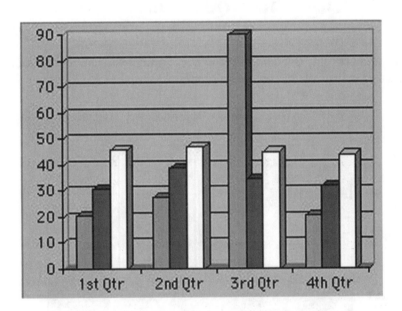

Line graphs are used to illustrate changes or growth rates over time.

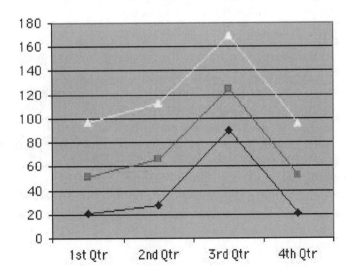

Various kinds of computer software can give you the ability to represent line graph information in dynamic ways, such as the *ribbon graph*.

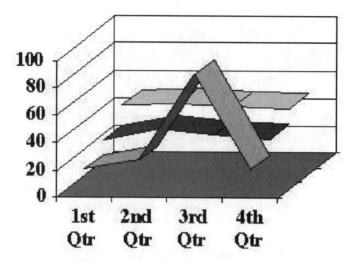

If you want to accentuate the differences in a line graph, you can fill in the spaces between the lines and create what's called a *mountain graph*.

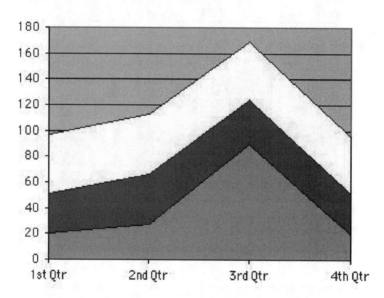

Many kinds of information are often presented on **posters**. If you're going to make a poster, use sturdy material. Thin poster board tends to bend easily and can fall off of an easel. Indeed, anything you can roll into a tube is probably a bad idea. Foam core (available at various arts and crafts stores) costs a little more but provides very sturdy material.

Handouts are often helpful, depending on your purpose for using them. You may want the audience to be able to follow along, and a handout not only allows them to do so; it also gives them a set of notes with which they can leave. You want to consider, however, whether handouts would be helpful or be a hindrance. For instance, audience members may pay more attention to the handout than to you. Similarly, they can become noisy and distracting when people pass them around as you speak. Even if you provide handouts at the end of your presentation, they can become distracting for the student who speaks after you.

Presentations have often traditionally used **slide shows**. Slides can be of the standard 35 mm variety, but you can now do more sophisticated types of slide presentations using computers and software such as Microsoft PowerPoint. These kinds of presentations allow you to incorporate images, sounds, movies, fancy text, text that moves, etc. Despite the programming capabilities of such software, always be careful not to let the slide show steal the show.

Overhead transparencies are also a commonly-used form of visual aid. You can have these made at various photocopy stores, or you can make them yourself by buying overhead transparency material from any office supply store. If making them yourself, be certain to buy the right materials. Some are made for ink jet printers, some for laser printers, and some for photocopy machines. Using the wrong material in a machine will create a mess. If using overheads, be certain to leave about a 1" border around the edges of the transparency. If you place material all the way to the edge, it may get cut off once it's actually on the overhead projector.

Students often ask how to use an overhead projector. Very simply, if you're facing the audience and the projector is pointing its light behind you, just place the overhead on the machine so that you can read it. (It's no different than if you set a piece of paper on the machine in order to read it. But don't use paper; you need transparent material.) You'll also want to look for an on/off button.

Video (or DVD) can be used to show clips from movies, television shows, home video, etc. If using video, be certain it's cued up to the proper starting point. You don't want to waste the audience's time while you're fast-forwarding and rewinding to figure out where the tape is supposed to begin. Also, keep the clips short and to-the-point. Ideally, provide a brief explanation of what to watch or listen for prior to playing it; material of this kind doesn't always speak for itself.

Similarly, you can use **pre-recorded music** from tapes or CDs. As with video, you should give the audience some idea of what to listen for prior to playing it, and you should keep your selections short and to-the-point. Do not assume that you can use up 5 minutes of a 6-minute speech simply by playing music!

You might also have **pre-recorded oration**, such as excerpts from famous speeches. Again, provide some explanation of what to listen for prior to playing it.

> *Note, by the way, that using a chalkboard or markerboard as your visual aid is often a poor substitute for the work it takes to construct and craft a good visual. Unless circumstances call for it, avoid using these two media for your speech presentation aids.*

Why Use Presentation Aids?

In addition to simply adding interest, presentation aids serve a number of functions for an audience. First, they help you to **emphasize key points**. Focus presentation aids on what you want the audience to remember. Some presenters will tend to have a visual aid for nearly every word they say, but this tends to diminish the effectiveness of visual aids; everything seems to be getting the same amount of emphasis.

Second, visual aids can be used to help **break down complex information**. For instance, if you were talking about the cycles of a relationship, it would be helpful if you could show the audience a chart or overhead that illustrated the actual cycles.

Presentation aids are also beneficial to audience members with different **learning styles**. People tend to learn information best by using certain senses or modes of thinking. For example, a visual learner is someone who needs to literally see information in order to best comprehend it. Auditory learners need to hear information in order to comprehend. Kinesthetic learners are those who need to use their bodies to learn, such as active note-takers.

Also, people can use a combination of learning styles, such as visual-auditory learners. As such, if you were to only delivery your speech aurally, you could end up being less effective with the visual learners in your audience. By providing material in different modes—at least both orally and visually—you enhance the chances of reaching more audience members.

Rules for Using Presentation Aids

When using visual or other presentation aids, you need to follow certain rules in order to ensure that they work properly. Most of these are pretty straightforward, but it's sometimes amazing how speakers overlook even the simplest matters. In no particular order, here are common rules to follow:

- <u>Visual aids reinforce the spoken word</u>. A presenation aid must enhance your speech. Use it only if it makes your speech better. In any event, you should be able to deliver your presentation fairly effectively regardless of whether you have presentation aids.

- <u>Have one idea per visual aid</u>. Don't try to cram everything onto one poster board or overhead transparency. If you have something with a list on it, such as an overhead, reveal one idea at a time (e.g., cover the overhead with a piece of paper and gradually reveal one line at a time.)

- <u>Use words or short phrases</u>. In most cases, you don't want the audience engaged in an in-depth reading task. Just provide the most basic information and allow the oral part of your speech to provide the fine details. Information should presented in a manner that allows for quick and easy comprehension.

- <u>Keep the visual aid up long enough for comprehension</u>. Despite the fact that you want quick and easy comprehension, you still have to give the audience sufficient time to understand the information. In particular, if you use words, you can follow the rule used in broadcasting when they show words on television: leave it up long enough so that someone can read it out loud twice. (You should also use this technique as part of your rehearsal with the visual.)

- <u>Rehearse with the presentation aids</u>. Using presentation aids takes time, and you need to be proficient with exactly what you want to do when giving the actual presentation. If necessary, create mock equipment with which to practice. For instance, even if you don't have an overhead projector at home, you can still set up a box and pretend it's a projector. Put your overhead on the box at the appropriate point in the speech, remove it when done, etc.

- <u>Use the presentation aid only at the moment it's needed</u>. Otherwise, keep it out of sight. If you bring a visual aid into view too quickly, the audience might not realize it's not being used yet. They'll listen to what you're saying, look at the visual, and try to put the two together even though they don't belong together. They'll end up confused.

- <u>Remove the visual aid when done</u>. Similarly, if you leave the visual aid up after you're done with it, the audience might not realize you're done. Again, they'll try to link what you're saying with what they're seeing and end up confused.

- <u>Talk to the audience, not to the visual aid</u>. By the time you give your speech, you should know your material well. For instance, if you use a poster, you should know exactly what it says. There is no need for you to look at it while it's being used. Focus, instead, on your audience. They'll eventually look away from the visual and back at you, and it's nice if you're already making eye contact with them.

- <u>Explain the visual aid clearly</u>. Don't assume it speaks for itself. If you're showing numbers, etc., explain what all of it means.

- Label all information clearly. Make certain lettering, etc. is of a sufficient size, width, etc. that it stands out nice and neat. On posters, try to print with letters that are at least 2 inches high. With overheads, try to use a font size that's at least $1/4$ inch tall. (Don't go by font size. A 12-point font, for instance, can be really huge or really tiny depending on the font used). Whenever possible and appropriate, use a word processor rather than using handwriting.

- The visual must be large enough for everyone to see. The best measure of this is to determine the distance between you and the people in the back row. Then observe your visual aid from that distance and determine if you can see it.

- Use bold, distinct, primary colors. You might even consider outlining various colors with black lines, to make them stand out more. Remember, your images have to communicate quickly and be highly visible to all audience members. Primary colors (Red, Green, Blue) work best for quick visibility.

- Don't block the view. Again, during your rehearsal, determine where you'll be moving in relation to the placement of the visual aid. Make certain you're not going to stand in front of the poster, etc.

- Make sure all materials are in the proper order. If you have more than one overhead, poster, etc., you don't want to spend your time in front of the audience searching for the proper materials. Don't be messy, and you won't look messy.

- Make sure all video or audio is cued properly. As noted earlier, you don't want to waste time fast-forwarding or rewinding in front of the audience. If you have several video or audio clips, try to create one master tape (or CD) with all of the clips in the proper order, so that you don't have to keep popping tapes in and out of the machine.

- Evaluate the appropriateness of handouts. This doesn't mean never to use them, although they're usually not recommended for a public speaking course. Again, the question is whether they'll be useful or distracting. If distracting, avoid their use. Remember, also, that if you give handouts at the end of your speech, they may still be distracting during the next student's speech if people read them or pass them around at that point.

- Isolate key numbers on charts and tables. Students sometimes simply photocopy massive charts of information from books or other sources and present this as a visual aid, even though they intend only to refer to a few numbers among the many. Use a highlighter pen or a laser pointer to point these out to the audience. Better yet, take only the vital information you want and create a poster or overhead of your own with the information.

- Make certain poster board is sturdy enough to stand up without falling over or curling up. Again, consider using foam core, which is available at most arts and crafts stores.

- Prepare the audience for controversial materials. If you have graphic images or controversial audio materials, give your audience a warning. It's always best to consult with your professor or instructor prior to using such materials.

- Know the technology. The day of your speech is not the day to learn how to operate a VCR. Know what you're doing and respect your limits.

- Expect technical problems. Things go wrong. VCRs eat tapes. Bulbs burn out in overhead projectors. Computers crash. You need to anticipate that these things could happen and have a "Plan B" ready to go in case you can't use your visual aids as expected.

- Have a backup disk for multimedia presentations. If you're going to use PowerPoint, etc., you want to have at least two copies. You never know when your floppy disk will act funny on you, or when the CD you burned will fail to function properly.

- Make certain all necessary equipment is available. There's no point in creating the world's greatest PowerPoint presentation if a computer and projector will not be handy. Not every classroom is equipped with a computers, or DVD players, etc. Always check with your professor or instructor to determine if equipment is or can be made available.

- <u>Respect design principles</u>. Although an entire course could be devoted to how to properly design visual materials, there are at least a few principles you can put into practice now:

Maintain Visual Balance

Imagine that your image is sitting atop a balancing point. Then consider the relative size and proportions of people, objects, etc. that are on each side of the image. For example, the following image would be considered to be out of balance because the image on the left side is much larger than the image on the right:

To make the image more balanced, we might add more items to the right side of the image:

Typically, you'll want to maintain balance in your picture, although a deliberately imbalanced picture can give the image a more dynamic quality.

Distribute Images Along Major Axes

Imagine putting a grid over your image by dividing your image into nine boxes. You generally want to place text on or near the lines and place objects on or near the intersection points on the grid. NOTE: Do not actually draw a grid on your visual aid! Work with an imaginary grid.

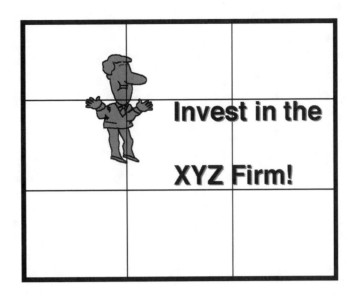

Work with "Z" Patterns

In Western culture, we read from top-to-bottom and left-to-right. You should distribute any objects in your image along this same kind of path.

TIP: Objects placed near the lower-right corner seem to command the most visual attention. If you have some image, word, or phrase to which you especially want the audience to pay attention, locate it near that vicinity.

EXERCISES

1) Your instructor will show a number of different types of visual aids and ask you to evaluate them in light of the rules for visual aids discussed in this chapter. For each visual aid, determine if it appears to be effect, be prepared to explain why or why not, and offer specific suggestions for improving the visual.

2) Your instructor will provide you with a sample speech. In small groups, discuss the speech and make recommendations as to where visual aids might best work in the speech. Also recommend what type(s) of visual aid should be used, and why. Given time and resources, try designing a small-scale poster that might be used.

9 *Language*

Term to Know

- Sapir-Whorf Hypothesis
- Linguistic Determinism
- Linguistic Relativity
- Denotative Meaning
- Connotative Meaning
- Inclusive Language
- Hedges
- Tag Questions
- Marking

"Sticks and stones may break my bones but names will never hurt me."

—*Childhood Adage*

We all can remember that childhood chant about "sticks and stones." Of course, even in childhood we learned that words and names can be painful. Language has the power to impact listeners. Words share knowledge but when chosen effectively can inspire, build trust, raise concern, build frustration and have a positive or a negative impact. The notion that words only serve a decorative purpose is surely an outdated concept. Language is not ornamental, words are power. The power of language becomes amplified when contextualized into the realm of public speaking. You have already learned of the ethical responsibilities that one has when engaging in public speaking so this chapter will offer theory and tips for you to be an ethical and effective communicator.

Language plays such a key role in our social interactions that language is truly a universal form of communication. However, while all cultures use words to communicate, language is unique to each culture. American linguists Edward Sapir and Benjamin Lee Whorf, developed the Sapir-Whorf hypothesis which focuses on the role of language and culture. The **Sapir-Whorf hypothesis** can be broken down into two basic principles: linguistic determinism and linguistic relativity. **Linguistic Determinism** is the idea that the language we use determines the way in which we view and think about the world around us. **Linguistic Relativity** supposes that the distinctions in one language are unique to that language alone. That people who speak different languages perceive and think about the world quite differently. For example, think about how living in Las Vegas impacts our language and in turn our culture. Certainly anyone living and driving in Las Vegas for even a short period of time is familiar with local lingo like "the spaghetti bowl" (The space where Interstate 15 and Interstate 95 meet), "D.I." (Desert Inn), "Trop" (Tropicana boulevard—not the hotel), and parts of town like Summerlin, Green Valley and Henderson. The unique aspects of gaming in our city also afford many of us to be familiar with free parking most everywhere, valet service and gaming terms like "comp" (short for free or complimentary), "eye in the sky" (the plentiful hidden cameras on the ceilings on every gaming room where all gaming tables are monitored) and "tip" or "toke" (gratuity) and many more. Knowing these terms and their correct meaning become important if we are to effectively communicate with others who share our culture as well as those who are removed from it. Adding to the possible confusion is that even though two people may know the same word they may interpret the meaning of that term differently. Words have two kinds of meaning: denotative and connotative.

Denotative Meaning is like a dictionary definition, it strives to be direct, objective and explicit. The Denotative meaning of a dog is canine. **Connotative Meaning** is personal, subjective and full of the feelings and emotion we inject into our understanding of something. The connotative meaning of a word would depend on your personal experiences. The connotative meaning of dog might be a soft, fluffy loveable pet, or could be a cruel, scary and deadly beast. Recognizing the intended meaning of your words is the first step toward harnessing the power of language.

Oral versus Written Communication

While acknowledging the significance of word selection and the unique role that language plays in communication we must also recognize the mode of communication will also affect language choice. Written communication has different rules than oral communication. Reading an essay reading an essay is not the same as giving a speech. Below is a list of six distinct qualities of language for an oral presentation.

1) **Contractions** are more acceptable in speeches than essays or other forms of written communication. Using we've (we have), don't (do not) and other contractions help the speaker appear more conversational.

2) **Personal pronouns** (I, you, we, and our) help the audience feel as though they are being *talked with* rather than *spoken to*.

3) **Colloquial words** are more acceptable. Using more familiar and less formal terms help the audience feel more at ease and also functions to increase the conversational quality of your presentation.

4) **Shorter sentences** are important in oral communication for two reasons: they help the listener stay focused on your message and increase comprehension of your ideas, and shorter sentences will prevent you from becoming vocally exasperated by long, minimally punctuated sentences.

5) **Active voice** in your writing will keep the audience more interested than using the passive voice.

6) **Judicious word selection** is important as you are writing for the ear, not the eye. Readers can go back and reread a passage for clarification; listeners cannot so you must choose your words wisely, and with intention.

7) **Time versus Space:** Because your presentation is being orally presented to, rather than read by, an audience you must ensure that your terms are appropriate to that context. For example, when referencing another point in your speech you must use "time terms" not "spatial" terms. A piece of information was stated "earlier" or "before" not "above." You might be coving an issue "next" or "later" but not "below."

Incorporating these differences between oral and written language can help ensure that your speech will have the appropriate verbal construction. Beyond the specifics associated with language used in an oral presentation thee re some general guidelines for language that you should follow. Below is a list guiding principles to follow.

Guiding Principles for Language

Clarity: Your language should strive to avoid ambiguity. Your language should be as clear as possible. Avoid too much technical jargon with untrained audiences (e.g., "the RAM in my CPU is insufficient to make a proper connection at this IP address, thus leading me to consider a different PPP protocol"). If jargon has to be used with an unfamiliar audience be sure to explain the terms. Try to use lay language whenever possible.

Concreteness: Avoid abstract statements. Your language should be as specific and concrete as possible. Recall that you want to ensure that you audience understand your intended meaning of the words used. Avoid vague descriptions like "many", "a lot," "most" or "a large amount," try to quantify the amount using numbers or precise information. See the chart showing the transition from abstract to concrete.

Abstract   Concrete

Animal- - - - - - - - Mammal - - - - - - - - Feline - - - - - - - - Persian cat - - - - - - - - My cat Henry

Accuracy: When conducting research make sure you research unfamiliar words. A fast way to lose credibility in front of your audience is to misuse a concept by using a word that you do not fully understand. A dictionary is a great tool to help you understand the meaning and pronunciation of a word.

Description: Select language that can invoke sensory images. Appeal to the five senses (sound, sight, touch, taste and smell) by using emotionally charged language that is vivid, detailed and memorable. Think of poetry's ability to invoke so much emotion with so few words. Good description will help your audience retain the information you are presenting. For example, which description is more memorable? "That guy is really ugly" or "It looks like his face caught on fire, and someone put it out with a fork." The latter statement is graphic to sure, but it shows how descriptive language can leave an lasting impression.

Cultural Sensitivity: Considering the power of language it is important to avoid marginalizing your audience Use audience analysis skills to better understand your audience and have the language reflect that audience. Make sure the language avoids stereotyping people based on gender, race, religion, physical ability or other demographic factors. The use of sexist, racist, ageist or other discriminatory language is likely to ostracize your audience.

Inclusive Language: Your language should strive to include your audience and not ostracize them. In addition to using plural pronouns like "we" and "our" consider other ways that your language can reflect a desire to incorporate the audience. Don't marginalize your audience by talking to them about "their" problem or how "they" should follow certain solution steps as such language contextualizes you s an outsider and that will lower your ability to inspire identification in your audience.

Assertive Language: Convey confidence and conviction in your language. Some speakers covey weakness through their word choice through the use of qualifiers. There are two types of weak language to guard against: hedges and tag questions. **Hedges** are unnecessary words or phrases that qualify or introduce doubt into your own words. For example, "I may not be right, but…" or "I guess my position is…" Notice how these words can create doubt in the audience's mind. **Tag Questions** appear at the end of a statement and turn an assertive statement into a questioning comment. For example, "McDonald's has the best tasting french fries, right?" or "this proposal is too expensive, don't you think?"

AVOID Marking: **Marking** means adding gender, race sexual orientation, age or other identifier unnecessary to the verbal description. For example, "Dr. Adams is the best *female* doctor I know." Adding the gender identifier is not only irrelevant, worse it may function to trivialize her work. Audience members may interpret your statement to mean that Dr. Adams is a good doctor, *for a woman,*" whether or not that was the intended meaning.

Memorable Imagery

As discussed previously, using descriptive language is an effective tool in making your speech memorable. While that section discussed how you use descriptive words to make your speech enduring, you can expand that idea to making memorable phrases full of potent imagery. There are three primary techniques based in figurative language that you should consider.

1. **Simile**: An <u>explicit</u> or direct comparison between two or more dissimilar things, usually using the words "like" or "as." For example, "the rocks rolled down the hill knocking down trees and bushes like a bowling ball knocking down pins" or "slow *as* molasses."

2. **Metaphor**: An <u>implied</u> or indirect comparison between two unlike things made without using "like" or "as." For example, "Great idea Tom, you hit a home run with that marketing proposal." Here we see how metaphor can illustrate how strong Tom's marketing pitch was by using a baseball metaphor of a "home run." Metaphors can help audiences comprehend abstract concepts by comparing to concrete things. Be cautious with employing overused metaphors and similes (fit as a fiddle; busy as a bee; light as a feather).

3. **Personification**: Attributing human qualities to an inanimate things or events. For example, "the rain danced on the car window" or "the voice of democracy." Personification can breathe life into lifeless objects and add to the potency of that imagery.

Rhythmic Language

Another way to help your speech have a lasting effect on the audience is to use rhythm in your speech. This does not mean that each sentence in your speech should rhyme; after all, this isn't an Eminem rap. However, you can integrate certain phrases with imagery that serves a mnemonic function. Below is a discussion of four techniques based in figurative language that you may consider utilizing.

1. **Alliteration**: Alliteration is the repetition of sounds at the beginning of words that are near one another. For example, "Paul's painted pottery is on sale today!") When used sparingly it can catch the listeners' attention and help make the speech memorable. (For another example, consider the title of this book!).

2. **Antithesis**: Antithesis is combination of contrasting ideas in the same sentence. Antithesis works through the juxtaposition of contrasting ideas. Place words and phrases in contrast or opposition to one another. One of the best known antitheses is John F. Kennedy's famous quotation, "ask not what your country can do for you—ask what you can do for your country."

3. **Onomatopoeia**: This linguistic device operates through the use of words that sound like the thing they stand for. Consider words that imitate natural occurring sounds like "buzz," "crack," or "hiss."

4. **Parallelism**: Arrangement of related words adding to the rhythm through balanced arrangement. The film <u>Forrest Gump</u> offers an example of parallelism in the phrase "*stupid is* as *stupid does*."

EXERCISES

1) A conclusion to this chapter might read:

> Language plays a crucial role in the construction and presentation of a successful speech. This chapter has explored a number of features of verbal communication in hopes of illustrating ways for you to harness the power of language and ride it to an effective end. Potent and persuasive presentations are built with various linguistic devices to improve listeners' comprehension and retention of central ideas.

See if you can locate which of the guidelines and tips for memorable and rhythmic language were used. Circle which concepts were used:

Personification   Metaphor   Simile

Parallelism   Alliteration   Onomatopoeia   Antithesis

2) Much of our language has historically contained a sexist bias. The politically correct movement has strived to incorporate gender neutral terms to remove any gender prejudice. Below is a list of words, can you link of new or alternative word that removes the gender while still conveying the same meaning?

Old Term	New Term
1. Policeman	1. _____
2. Fireman	2. _____
3. Mailman	3. _____
4. Poetess	4. _____
5. Comedienne	5. _____
6. Garbage man	6. _____

10 *Delivery*

Terms to Know

- Presentation setting
- Physical environment
- Social themes
- Social roles and relationships
- Memorized speeches
- Manuscripts
- Impromptu speaking
- Extemporaneous speaking
- Conversational style
- Delivery notes
- Working outline
- Keyword approach

- Principles of note cards
- Card or page limit
- Rehearsal schedule
- Gestures
- Posture and Movement
- Eye contact
- Anchor points
- Facial expressions
- Vocal quality
- Contractions
- Appearance

Most of us want to make a good impression when in front of an audience. No doubt, the actual moment of delivering your speeches in this class is foremost on your mind. Certainly, you'll want to explore the chapter on dealing with your anxiety, and that's also a topic of this course. This chapter, however, is not devoted to the fears you may have. Rather, it focuses on the nature of ways to prepare for the actual delivery as well as the delivery itself.

As with most of the chapters in this book, you'll find that good delivery is not a simple process. That's not meant to intimidate you; it's simply a statement of fact. Giving a presentation takes work, and most speakers put a reasonable amount of effort into their practice in order to maximize their chances of a good experience for both themselves and their audiences. To better understand the nature of delivery, we'll look at the nature of the presentation setting, different types of delivery, methods of developing effective delivery notes, and overall presentation mannerisms such as gestures and eye contact.

Presentation Setting

One useful practice to follow when you know you're going to give a presentation is (if possible) to visit the site where you'll be speaking. Knowing the environment ahead of time can give you valuable clues that can help you anticipate what you may or may not be able to accomplish in your delivery. For instance, knowing that you'll be speaking in close quarters can tell you that you may not be able to walk around, and you can better adapt your approach to that presentation.

The **presentation setting** consists of three elements: the physical environment, the social themes at play, and the social roles and relationships to which you'll need to attend. The **physical environment** is just what it sounds like: it requires becoming aware of possible noise factors (maybe you need a microphone), seating arrangements, available technology (perhaps you want to use PowerPoint; perhaps there's no podium), your mobility (you may be expected to sit, or you may be expected to stand, or to walk), etc.

Social themes give you some idea about the formality of the occasion. You need to be able to label the type of situation in which you'll be presenting: is it a business meeting? a lecture? an inspirational talk at a special event? In some cases, there may be an expectation that you'll be very formal, with limited movements. In other instances, perhaps you'll want to be much more mobile and expressive.

Social roles and relationships give you information about how the interaction between you and audience is to take place. This information can give you some idea about what kind of stance and attitude you may want or need to take to your audience. Perhaps it's a salesperson/customer relationship; or teacher/student; or manager/employee; or co-workers of equal standing. You would, undoubtedly, speak and behave somewhat differently with an audience of potential customers than you would to a student or to co-workers. (The chapter on audience analysis can also be very useful to you in this regard.)

Types of Delivery

While you're assessing the nature of the occasion and its setting, you also have to determine a method of delivery. There are four primary methods of speech delivery: memorized, manuscript, impromptu, and extemporaneous. Each of these types is appropriate and even advantageous in certain situations.

A **memorized** speech is, of course, one in which you deliver without notes. This approach would, obviously, be quite advantageous if you wanted to be exceptionally direct with your audience and to convey a sense of knowledge and confidence. For instance, if you were giving a sales presentation, you might make a good impression by appearing to know all there is to know about what you're selling.

Of course, the primary disadvantage of memorizing speeches is that you might forget what you need to say. You had better be prepared for this contingency, if this is the approach you want to take. Even having notes handy (just in case) may not work; you may still end up having a long, noticeable pause in the delivery while you're rummaging through your notes to figure out where you need to be.

Another disadvantage is that you could end up sounding artificial. In a sense, you could end up sounding too rehearsed and too predictable. Your efforts to remember the words to say can begin to outweigh your actual attention to the audience.

Memorizing requires that you learn your speech by sections (introduction, body, and conclusion; see the chapter on organization). You also, clearly, will have to put in a lot of practice time.

A speech delivered by **manuscript** is one in which you read word-for-word from a speech written on paper. Clearly, this method is best if you absolutely cannot afford to forget to say something, or cannot afford to accidentally say something that could later become problematic. Politicians, for instance, often rely on manuscripts because what they say could end up literally being a matter of global consequence.

For most everyday speakers, the major downfalls of using manuscripts are that they are impersonal and can create an artificial sound. A manuscript, however well rehearsed, still tends to require that you give more attention to it than to your audience. Eye contact and gesturing are often more limited. You may end up projecting your voice downward while trying to read, thus make you less audible. Further, you can end up sounding more like you're "reading at" your audience than you are "talking to" them. If public speaking were a mere matter of just getting up in front of people and reading words off of paper, then there would be no need for public speaking classes. Giving presentations is more sophisticated than that.

If you are going to use a manuscript, you want to write the speech out completely. Type the manuscript in a font size that's large enough for you to read easily. Keep paragraphs small, roughly between 3 and 5 sentences. Underline or otherwise highlight words and phrases you want to emphasize. Be as familiar with the manuscript as possible, so as to provide as much eye contact as possible. Finally, when you do practice, be certain you practice speaking with the manuscript. You may find it challenging to do something as simple as turning pages, and you probably want to do that without drawing attention to it. (See the "Folder Technique" described later in this chapter.)

Impromptu speaking is what you do when you have little or no preparation time. In this speaking situation, either you are asked to speak "on the spot," or you know you'll be speaking soon but you're not certain what the topic will be about. If possible, once you know your topic, try to jot ideas on a note card or something similar (but inconspicuous). Also, if possible, practice with these notes.

Of course, time may not be possible. Regardless of whether you can prepare, there are certain immediate key principles to follow with impromptu speaking. More about these can be learned in the chapter on impromptu speaking and in the chapter on organization, but a few are discussed here.

First, open with impact; grab the audience's attention. Next, have a clear thesis and a specific preview of your claims. Then develop you main points, trying to use transitions and signposts to help you and your audience follow the pattern of your organization. Finally, review your main points, summarize your thesis, and close with impact.

Extemporaneous speaking is a final approach to speaking, and it's the one that is emphasized in this book and in this course. This method is somewhat of a middle-ground between memorized and manuscript speaking. **Extemporaneous speaking** involves the use of notes with words and short phrases (not word-for-word sentences) that prompt your memory as you continue to present your speech.

In extemporaneous speaking, you glance briefly at your notes, find the next word or phrase in your notes, then come back and talk to your audience. Because you don't have a word-for-word manuscript in front of you, you'll obviously have to rehearse this type of presentation carefully.

The advantages of extemporaneous speaking are that it can give you a natural, conversational tone and that you don't have to go through the difficulties of a completely memorized speech. Speakers who have a natural, **conversational style** are those who speak directly to their audience members in a straightforward tone. They exude a certain spontaneity that is present in everyday conversation.

This style makes sense in many speaking situations. Put yourself in the position of an audience member for a moment. Do you prefer speakers who appear to speak directly to you at times, and who appear to speak directly to other audience members as well? These are speakers who also exude a certain confidence that makes them seem real and that may enhance their credibility.

Another advantage of extemporaneous speaking is that you are able to use reminders throughout the presentation. Of course, some might see this as a disadvantage. It takes practice to learn which words and phrases you want to use, and you may have to make several revisions to your notes before you've developed what works best for you. Also, it clearly takes rehearsal to develop your understanding and familiarity of words and phrases. It can also initially be frustrating that you may not always say things the same way twice. Each rehearsal will have some differences in exactly how you say things.

The rest of this chapter is devoted to the extemporaneous style. First, however, let's briefly review the three major types of delivery:

Method	Description	Advantages	Disadvantages
Memorized	Uses few or no notes	You look and sound impressive and direct	You could forget material
Manuscript	A word-for-word rendition of what you'll say	You're less likely to forget material	You're less likely to sound natural and spontaneous; you could end up with a monotone
Impromptu	You have little or no preparation time	You're going to sound spontaneous and direct	You have to think on your feet and know the rules of organizing a speech on-the-spot
Extemporaneous	You use notes with words and short phrases only to prompt your memory	You can sound natural and conversational without having to completely memorize	It can take more time to prepare notes and rehearse

Developing Delivery Notes

The extemporaneous style of delivery allows you to use notes. These can be either on paper or on note cards. Note cards are often preferable, as they can be less distracting to the audience. Ultimately, your goal is to use notes as an aid and not as a security blanket. That means minimizing the number of pages or cards you use, and it means not trying to hold these up so high that you begin to put a physical barrier between you and your audience.

Ultimately, how you make your cards is up to you. They are, after all, your notes. Some people like to write notes to themselves, reminding them to pause, give emphasis, smile, etc.

Nonetheless, there are some fundamental rules you want to follow in order to make your notes reasonably workable for you. Those will be explored in just a moment. First, in order to better understand the nature of extemporaneous notes, let's compare the general appearance of three types of notes: a delivery outline using extemporaneous style, a full-sentence working outline, and a manuscript.

Note that your **delivery notes** need not necessarily be in outline form. As long as you understand what you're doing at any given moment in a speech, your notes can be in a very different form if that works for you.

The **working outline** is what you turn in to your instructor. More information about this outline is covered in the chapter on organization. Here, be aware that it's written in full-sentence form, and that the words you eventually say in your speech might not correspond exactly as what's written on paper. (We're talking here about differences in wording only. You still have to deliver all of the key information.)

Notice that all three of these types of notes convey the same information. As you get closer to the extemporaneous style, however, the notes become much more abstract. Your objective is to find a word or phrase that will prompt a rehearsed memory of what that particular word or phrase is about as well as what you wanted to say about it. No one can tell you what that word or phrase should be; you'll have to practice and experiment with what works well for you.

Delivery Outline (What you speak from)	Working Outline (What you turn in) *30 seconds*	Manuscript (What you don't use)
I. Introduction	I. Introduction	Some of you might remember the 1996 Olympics where Kerri Strugg won the Gold Medal in women's gymnastics. Let me just remind you of that event. [Show video clip]
A. Attention Device: Kerri Strugg	A. Attention Device: Video story of Kerri Strugg	
B. Audience Orientation: 1. Typical example 2. Surprised by how much	B. Audience Orientation: 1. This is a typical example of how media often distort information. 2. Although we should be concerned, I'm frequently surprised by how much power we think the media have to control us.	What most of you don't know is that the media lied about it. First of all, the U.S. Team was not the last to go; no one knew what was needed to win the gold medal, and Strugg wasn't under that kind of pressure. Second, they knew she was not injured permanently, yet they acted as if they were as uncertain as us. In short, they re-edited the event and withheld information.
C. Speech Purpose: 1. Hope to persuade 2. Audience control	C. Speech Purpose: I hope today to persuade you that we—as audience members—actually have greater control than we are led to believe.	This is a typical example of how the media—even the news—often distort information. It's because of these kinds of actions that we're now witnessing campaigns to limit what media can and can't say. Although there is justification for concern, there is equal justification to suggest that media might not have the level of power we want to grant them.
D. Background: 1. Powerful effects 1930s a. Payne - legacy of fear b. Comics 2. Banning content bad a. Other approaches b. First Amendment	D. Background : 1. "Powerful effects" has been our most common belief since the 1930s a. Payne film studies looked at new medium of film (1) Educators claimed it threatened youth (2) Claimed it had very powerful effects (3) Gave birth to "legacy of fear" [DeFleur, 1990] b. Followed by a similar comic book scare in 1950s 2. But trying to ban media content on the basis of these studies is dangerous. a. There are other viewpoints and types of research. b. Outright bans threaten First Amendment rights.	At least, anyway, media audiences have much more power than is thought, and I hope today to persuade you that we—as audience members—actually have greater control than we are led to believe. Most of our fears about these "powerful effects" can be traced to the Payne move studies of the 1930s. The new medium of film scared many educators, who claimed it threatened our youth and had very powerful effects. This study gave birth to what Melvin DeFleur has termed the "legacy of fear." This fear showed itself again in the 1950s when comic books were seen as the next big threat. [etc.]

Now that you have an idea of what goes on a note card, there are a few tips to follow that can make your cards work for you rather than against you. Take a look at the following note card. It's an example of a good card, and several good **principles of note cards** can be seen in it:

- Start by underlining key words and phrases in your outline. Copy all of those onto note cards, keeping the following provisions in mind.
- Limit card size to 3" x 5" index cards, one side only. Put your name on the other side of each card.
- Write clearly for yourself. Write large enough so that you can read it if holding the card at waist level. Make sure your writing is legible—type or word-process your cards if need be.
- Leave space to make it readable
- Try to use different note card for each of the three primary sections of your speech (Introduction, Body, Conclusion).
- Write out any quotations or statistics.
- Include source citations on your cards (see the chapter on Research)
- Use words and short phrases only
- Number each card
- Have only one idea per line
- Never continue wording from one card to another—finish each card with a complete thought
- If it's useful, you might also want to color-code your cards using marker pens to identify various parts of the speech and changes you'll want to make when they arise
- You might also write delivery cues and other notes to yourself on your cards, such as "Slow Down," "Breathe," "Move to Next Point," "use Visual Aid"; etc.
- Draw lines to create sections of information (probably no more than 4 sections per card)
  - This has the effect of creating a lot of small "cards" on a single card
  - When you refer back to your notes, you need only find the section you left, rather than searching through the entire card

Drawing lines to create sections of information allows you to treat each section as a "mini" card. When you refer back to your notes, you need only find the section where you left off and search through that smaller amount of information. Try to have no more than 4 sections (3 lines) per card.

Note that this card is not written in an outline format. This type of card follows what's called a "**keyword**" approach. The previously-illustrated card doesn't have any labels to go with the information, but you may find it helpful to also label the different parts of your card. For example, look at how the following converts a full-sentence introduction from a working outline into a keyword outline for a note card:

Example of a full-text introduction:
"**Introduction:** It has been described as the one true form of American music. I am not talking about Rock n' Roll or even Hip Hop. I am speaking of Jazz. Musicologist Golden Swenson says that Jazz is the only true American form of music. As fans of music it is important that we know about this important genre of music **Thesis:** Today, I'm going to share information about Jazz that may surprise you. **Preview:** First, I'm going to talk about the history of Jazz, then I'll discuss some major figures in the evolution of Jazz, net we'll examine break off Jazz styles, and finally, workplace we'll explore the types of music that have been influenced by Jazz."

Example of a key word introduction:

"**Introduction:** American music … Not Rock or Hip Hop … Musicologist Golden Sweneson one true. American music
We're all fans   Need to know more **Thesis:** Jazz. **Preview:** history…
Major figures … Jazz styles Modern influences"

You should also have a **card or page limit**. On average, you can expect to develop about 3 cards for every 5 minutes of speaking. However, you don't want to overdo it. After all, you don't want to end up shuffling an entire deck of cards up there. For longer speeches, you'll need to be especially adaptive and work to limit the maximum number of cards to about 10.

Numerous sheets of paper can also cause problems, such as becoming disorganized or noisy. As such, try to have no more than two sheets of paper that can lie side by side on the lectern. Apply a LARGE font—try a 18-point Times font to see an example:

Introduction: <u>"**Introduction:**</u> American music … Not Rock or Hip Hop … Musicologist Golden Sweneson. one true. American music	**Main Pt:** Jazz History … **1920s** … Edward Shank, Ph.D., "History of Jazz" … 1930s … changes 1940s.. innovations. 1950s … recognition

Excerpts of key word outline on two sheets of paper. Envision a large font size. No squinting!

Lectern

You may find it impossible to place a key word outline in large font on two sheets of paper. You may need three or four pages. For a more streamlined, professional approach, consider using a 3-ring binder.

The binder works well for several reasons. First, you'll deal only with a single unit at the lectern instead of several cards or sheets of paper. Also, the binder allows you to flip through the various pages with ease. (For increased ease put pages in clear plastic sleeves called "slip sheets.") Finally, the package looks professional and organized.

Setting the Rehearsal Schedule

At last, your notes are developed and you're ready to rehearse. As part of your rehearsal, you have to learn more than just the words you'll say. There are also a number of rehearsal principles that need to be followed. Once you read through this section, you'll probably realize that you don't want to wait until the night before the speech to begin rehearsing it. "Rehearsal" is more than just practicing words.

You want to begin by establishing a **rehearsal schedule**. From the moment you are assigned the date you'll speak, you should dig out a calendar and begin developing a strategy. Anticipate that you'll probably want to begin rehearsing at least one week before the speech, if that's possible. Then take the remaining time and devote about 1/2 of it to research and 1/2 to organizing and writing the working outline. As part of the latter, anticipate time needed to write a proper works cited page and to translate the working outline into a set of keyword delivery notes. Work backward from the date you're scheduled to speak, and write the key events (e.g., "Start rehearsal today") on the appropriate dates. Strive to follow that schedule or get ahead of it if possible.

General Rehearsal Principles

With each rehearsal in which you engage, there are also a few practices you want to follow. First, <u>anticipate devoting at least an hour of practice to every minute you'll speak</u>. You may need more or less, depending on your familiarity with the material.

Also, <u>as part of your rehearsal, you want to practice only with the keyword outline.</u> Do <u>not</u> practice with a manuscript or full-sentence outline.

In addition, <u>practice rehearsing manageable chunks of information</u>. Some speakers take an ineffective approach, wherein they like to start at the beginning and work their way through the speech until they hit some snag. They fix it, start over, and continue working toward the conclusion. When they finally get to the conclusion, they stop.

The problem is, using this approach, they end up rehearsing some parts more than others. The closer they get to the conclusion, the less likely they will have properly rehearsed that material.

A better approach is to <u>learn a small section of material at a time</u>. Rehearse only that section until you have at least a working familiarity with it (e.g., the first 30 seconds). Then go to the next small section of information and do the same (e.g., the next 30 seconds). Then combine these two sections into one (e.g., the first minute). Continue to add other sections in the same way (rehearse the section first and then add it) until you're done.

<u>Always rehearse out loud</u>. You cannot rehearse sitting in a chair and saying the presentation to yourself. It must be out loud, at full volume, and at the pace you intend to speak. Otherwise, your actual timing will suffer.

<u>Strive for the "middle time" if given a time range</u>. For example, if you're giving a speech that runs between 7 and 9 minutes, try to time your speech at 8 minutes. Students sometimes report that, when they were home, they had their speech "timed at exactly 7 minutes," yet when they give the actual speech, it comes out longer than that. One reason for this may be that, when in front of an actual audience, we unconsciously adjust ourselves to our perceptions of how quickly the audience is responding to our words. We end up slowing down, so to speak, to match the audience's pace.

In any event, you must <u>respect time limits</u>. All speeches must have time limits in order for speaking occasions to function properly.

Finally, <u>determine the pronunciation of names and terms with which you may be unfamiliar and prepare a pronunciation of them</u>. Nothing is a bigger giveaway that you did not rehearse than if you struggle with pronunciation during the speech. It raises the question of why you didn't encounter that name or word until that moment, or why you didn't prepare for it during rehearsals.

If you can't determine a proper pronunciation, you can always introduce it by saying "I believe this is pronounced . . ." If helpful, you can also write these phonetically on your delivery notes.

Physical Factors

Having prepared your notes and establishing your schedule, you'll want to practice various forms of movement and audience contact. These include gestures, body positioning, eye contact, facial expressions, voice quality, use of contractions, and appearance.

The use of **gestures** is meant to emphasize important points and clarify ideas. Faulty hand gestures often result from nervousness and can detract from your speech. Your hands should rest comfortably at your sides when not used for emphasis. When you do gesture, do so above waist level and above the lectern when used. Note, however, that if you're holding note cards, you don't want to raise them much above waist level so as to avoid making them too obvious.

Dos and Don'ts of Gestures

Things to Do

- Make gestures above your waist.

- Makes gestures distinct

- Gesture with Intention and purpose

- Balance between each hand (unless notecards are being held in one hand)

Things to Avoid

- Fidget with fingers, arms, clothing or jewelry

- Put hands in pockets

- Play with coins or keys in pants

- Lock fingers together

- Clamp hands onto podium

- Tap Podium

Speaking of movements, you also want to pay attention to your **posture and movement**. Your body should be relaxed and comfortable during your speech. Here are some tips to help you:

- Take a deep breath as you leave your seat and approach the podium or front of the room.
- Stand tall and stride to the lectern or front of the room confidently.
- Position yourself so you can see the entire audience. If you plan to leave the lectern, make sure you have a clear path on each side.
- Do not have to begin speaking the second you reach the lectern or front of the room. Take a couple of seconds for yourself. Establish brief eye contact with your audience. Then begin.

Dos and Don'ts of Posture and Movement

Things to Do

- Bend your knees a little. Locking your legs back will cut off your circulation and you will risk passing out or losing your balance.

- Toes should point toward the audience.

- Feet should parallel and be shoulder width apart

- Move on transitions

- Walk normally (no sidesteps, babysteps or the electric slide)

- Realize that podiums do not hide your feet

Things to Avoid

- Lean on Podium

- Swaying back to front or side to side

- Stand on tiptoes

- Stand too close or too far away from audience

- Wear sandals or flip-flops

One of the most significant aspects of delivery is eye contact. **Eye contact** should be direct, sustained, distributed, and dominant. To be direct means to actually look into someone's eyes. When speaking to a small group, your goal is to look at each person briefly. Meet everyone's eyes for a second. When speaking to a larger group, balance your eye contact to all areas of the room.

You also want to bond with your audience even before you start speaking by *looking* at them! Establishing eye contact helps your credibility and can reduce your nervousness. In particular, it can help you find anchor points. **Anchor points** are friendly faces in the audience; they are the people who tend to smile and nod approval and other happy thoughts in your direction. You can often find them in an audience. Try looking for someone on the right side of the room, someone in the middle, and someone on the left. During those times when you might have a bit more anxiety, talk to them a bit more.

Eye contact also needs to be sustained. You want to hold direct eye contact with any one person for at least 1/2 second to a second. Don't engage in a stare-down and scare your audience away! But make it clear that you're actually making contact.

To be distributed means to ensure that you're speaking to all parts of the audience. You need to make noticeable efforts—including moving your head and neck—to make it clear that you're trying to speak to all members of the audience (for smaller audiences). Don't just speak to the center of the room and shift your eyes back and forth.

Dos and Don'ts of Eye Contact

Things to Do	• Make eye contact with a few members of the audience before you start your speech
	• Make a visual connection with audience members
Things to Avoid	• Stare at audience members for extended periods of time
	• Scan the audience robotically
	• Being so dependent on your notes that your eye contact is minimal or absent. This isn't a class in "speech reading."
	• Look over the audiences heads

Finally, you want eye contact to be dominant. That is to say, you want to strive for direct, sustained, and distributed eye contact at least 80% of the time or more. Remember, eye contact is not just "looking up a lot." It means making real contact.

Facial expressions are another concern. Your **facial expressions** should appear congenial and relaxed. They should also match your speech content and the tone of your presentation; for example, don't grin when talking about child abuse.

Finally, you want to focus on your **vocal quality**. Practice speaking from the diaphragm, rather than the throat. As you continue speaking over time, this will help you to sustain a higher volume. And don't confuse good volume with screaming or shouting. You still have to sound conversational.

You also need to control your pitch. Pitch includes the lowness or highness of your voice. When you adjust your pitch higher or lower to emphasize certain words, this is called "inflection."

To bring your speech to life, you want to vary your inflections. Sound extemporaneous and conversational, not monotone. As you practice your speech, circle words on your outline that may be emphasized. Be sure to avoid "sing-songiness." Sometimes speakers will slip into a specific pattern of speaking and this can lull the audience.

The rate at which you speak is also significant. People have to be able to hear what you say and have a little time to understand it. You can certainly employ a quicker verbal pace if your subject lends itself to something exciting. Conversely, you can deliberately allow your words to linger to apply drama to a serious topic.

Regardless, you also need to insert pauses, particularly at certain crucial moments. For instance, when concluding your speech, you can apply verbal and nonverbal closure. Instead of saying "In conclusion…," pause briefly, then lower your pitch. You may then transition into your closing statements.

Pauses have myriad benefits for speakers. First, when strategically placed, pauses add drama to your speech. Second, pauses help signal transitions between your main points and conclusion. Finally, pauses give the audience a moment to enjoy a humorous point.

As you practice, be sure to avoid some of the following common problems with rate:

Dos and Don'ts of Vocal Qualities

Things to Do

- Appropriate volume: ensure the audience can hear you.

- Vocal Variety: try to be conversational

- Use Pausing effectively

- Practice saying difficult terms or words

Things to Avoid

- Racing through speech too quickly

- Speaking in a "sing-song" pattern

- Mispronouncing words

You also have to consider your diction, which is the clarity of your words. If you speak too quickly or too quietly, you can often end up slurring your words and creating confusion.

One way to begin developing good diction is to practice various speech exercises. For instance, broadcasters sometimes repeat phrases that challenge the facial muscles, such as "zeem-zoom" or "moo-me-mah-me-moh-me." You can also pick up any book or article and . . . read . . . it . . . out . . . loud . . . in . . . a . . . deliberately . . . slow . . . fashion. Try to emphasize every single syllable. Don't rush. Your objective is to become articulate.

Along with voice quality, you also have to consider using **contractions**. Speak the way you talk normally. For example, if you were talking to a friend, you'd probably say something like "it's a really nice day," rather than "it is a really nice day." If you don't use contractions, you're likely to sound a bit too formal and stodgy, as if you were merely reading a term paper at people. (This is not a course in public reading!)

There is one exception to the contractions rule. Phrases that end in "not" probably should not always be contracted, for two reasons. First, you might want to give certain emphasis to the "not" in order to reinforce your point, such as saying "we canNOT afford to ignore the consequence of this action!" Secondly, it can sometimes be easy for an audience to mishear you. If you say "we can't afford to do this," the audience might end up hearing you say "we can afford to do this."

Using contractions is often a rule that runs contrary to what you might have learned in an English composition course. Remember, however, that you're delivering information meant for a listening audience, not a reading audience, so the rules are often different. If need be, you might even want to write your working outline with contractions, so as not to forget to use them in the speech.

With all of this consideration on voice quality and wording, you also have to give some overall consideration to your **appearance**. This refers to how well you're dressed, how well you're groomed, and so on. It's assumed here that you want to try to look your best for speeches you give in this class. It's unreasonable to enforce a dress code, given problems with work schedules, etc., but there are at least some efforts you can make (tucking in a shirt, etc.). You can also avoid rude appearance problems, such as wearing a hat or chewing gum.

EXERCISES

1) In small groups, consider the following speech topics: A discussion about obsessive-compulsive disorders and an argument against the death penalty. Now, for each speech, discuss how a speaker who delivers that speech under different circumstances would have to adapt to those circumstances. How, for example, would the speaker's abilities to move, gesture, etc. be different if the same speech were given as a class presentation as opposed to a heated discussion over dinner with friends? How, also, might the speaker have to differ with and without the presence of a podium?

2) As a group, evaluate the following note cards in terms of how well they follow the principles of note cards. Make suggestions for improvements.

(4)

Common age 12 years.

Numbers rising - Older more expas

8th 30%   12th   55%

1 of 10 seniors use cocaine

Inhalants - 8th 20%, down 5%
                      in 12th

I have dissussed   ⑥

① Drugs problems in society

② ER accidents

③ highshools

④ Different regions effected

The claims of GM...unfounded/aren't supported

C. The final reason exposes how...GMF isn't nec.
  1. Miguel Altieri P@UCB points out...US...20-30 mal
  2. According to Peter Rosset expert w/h co-dir IFDP
    a. First, he states...grain 3,500-requires 2,500
    b. In fact, Rosset calculates...4.3 lbs of food
    c. Furthermore, he states...food prod isn't → poverty

With enough food...pop...millions still starving
  it's clear tech ie. GM isn't...feed the world

C. Background Material: Before I state my case, let me give you a little background information about this subject.

1. Long before the SUVs of today were even a concept, there were the crude, noisy and difficult to operate SUVs of the past such as the old Ford Bronco, International Scout and Toyota Landcruiser of the 60's and 70's. The Jeep Cherokee may have change all that since it's versatility combined with bulky styling appealed to soccer moms and dads unwilling to accept that they were really minivan material.

2. Todays SUVs are built with luxury and convenient items and has become much more civilized the than aforementioned SUVs of the past.

11 *Storytelling*

Terms to Know

- Narrative Paradigm
- Narrative Fidelity
- Narrative Coherence
- Story Climax and Resolution

Narrative Theory

Communication scholar Walter Fisher contends that human beings are inherently storytellers. That people "comprehend life as a series of ongoing narratives, as conflict stories with characters, beginnings, middles and ends[1]." Thus the lessons we have learned in life exist in the stories we relate. A well-constructed narrative can be equally informative and persuasive. In this speech you can develop a message that carries a moral or lesson you learned through a life experience. Stories can be dramatic or humorous.

Walter Fisher has developed a theory for understanding and evaluating stories called the **Narrative Paradigm**. The two main elements of the narrative paradigm are "narrative coherence" and "narrative fidelity." **Narrative Coherence** asks whether or not the stories events seem to make sense and do the characters act consistently. How well does the story hang together? Is the story logical? **Narrative Fidelity** measures if the story "rings true" to the listener's experience. Does the story strike a responsive cord with the life encounters of the audience. Simply put, the Narrative Paradigm argues that we listen to stories and weigh them favorably or unfavorably based on how the story coheres together and how well we identify with the characters and events of the tale.

---

[1] Griffin, Em. (2003). *Theory Communication: A First Look at Communication.* "Dramatism of Kenneth Burke". Fifth Edition. McGraw-Hill. New York. N.Y.

When crafting your Storytelling Speech be sure to apply the two dimensions of the **Narrative Paradigm** as it may help insure that your story is both logically constructed and likely to engage the audience. For further assistance in constructing your story examine the traditional story structure discussed below.

Story Structure

Most well put together stories follow a four-part structure:

1) **Opening:** Get your audience's attention and set the stage by giving the audience all necessary background information. Use descriptive language to draw a mental picture for your audience.

2) **Complication/Crisis:** Describe the primary difficulty or conflict that occurs in your tale. This will build the dramatic involvement of your audience.

3) **Climax:** Develop the complication to a culmination.

4) **Resolution:** Finish the story by coming to a complete and satisfying end. The moral, theme or lesson should be evident from the tale and need no further explanation.

Developing Your Speech

Knowing traditional story arrangement is helpful in creating an outline of your speech, now you are ready to follow our steps for success from coming up with your topic all the way to practicing your finished presentation. Here are six steps to guide you in the process.

1) **Brainstorm for a topic:** Think of an event that deeply affected you. Talk with friends or family to help you brainstorm of a story.

2) **Clarify your story:** Run through your story in your head or write it down. Eliminate information/details unrelated to your core theme/moral.

3) **Arrange your story:** Make sure your audience will be able to follow along with you. Tell the story to a friend, roommate, or family member and ask them what the theme/moral was. Make sure the story follows a clear chronological structure so that the listener can understand each point of your story easily.

4) **Create an effective opening and closing:** Grab the audience's attention. Try to relate the closing back to the opening statement so the story comes full circle.

5) **Prepare your note card (if allowed by your instructor):** Since this is "your" story you are probably already very familiar with it and most likely do not need any notes. If you do opt to write down notes only write down key words and phrases to trigger your memory in case you get lost.

6) **Practice:** Present your speech aloud in front of real people at least 4 times. It is important to use real people because having an audience will help you get a fair sense of moments when your class audience may laugh or applaud necessitating a vocal pause from you. Also, sometimes speakers talk faster or slower when in front of an audience. Be sure to time yourself when practicing to ensure that you are speaking for the allotted amount of time.

Possible Topics for your Storytelling Speech

- The best day of my life
- The worst day of my life
- The scariest dream I ever had
- The funniest thing I ever did
- My most embarrassing moment
- How I learned an important life lesson
- Birth of a child

- My bravest moment
- Overcoming my greatest fear
- Family vacation
- A trip I took to another culture
- My first love
- Relationship with my parents or siblings
- A Secret

EXERCISE 1

Storytelling Speech Brainstorming sheet

Fill in each box below with as many ideas as you can that could be used for your Storytelling speech.

Lessons Learned	People (who affected me)	Best Experiences
Activities/Hobbies	**Personal Goals**	**Values**

My topic first choice _____

My topic second choice _____

My topic third choice _____

12 *Informative Speaking* ⓣ

(most common form of speaking)

Terms to Know
• Speech of Description
• Speech of Demonstration
• Speech of Explanation
• Categorical Organization
• Chronological Organization
• Sequential Organization
• Spatial Organization

One of the hallmarks of public speaking is the Informative speech. Informative is the most common form of speaking, as its goal is to share or convey knowledge. Informative speakers create environments in which the speaker has expertise or knowledge that an audience needs or desires but does not already have. Note that the informative speech is designed to share knowledge or information but not to persuade your audience. Scholars of oral communication indicate that there is no such thing as a purely informative or persuasive speech. There are always elements of persuasion in informative speeches, for example, just by choosing a single topic out of the infinite number of subjects suggests that this one is more important or privileged. The key for informative speaking is to educate rather than advocate. Be cautious when using terms like "should," "ought," or "need" in your thesis, as these are red flags indicating that you might be crossing the line to persuasion.

Functions of Informative Speaking

There are <u>three</u> primary types of informative speaking: speeches of description, demonstration and explanation. Each of these performs a specific function of informative speaking. Below you will see a detailed description of each of these three types of informative speaking.

Speech of Description: This type of speech offers the audience a mental picture of a topic—an object, person, place, event or activity. Draw a picture with your words. For example, you might speak on a country you have traveled to, a work of art, or topography of the Las Vegas Strip.

Speech of Demonstration: This type of speech provides the audience with an explanation of a specific process. This is also known as a "how-to" speech. For example, you might show the audience how to prepare sushi, create a web page, perform CPR, wax a snowboard or bid on Ebay. Demonstrative speeches are very common because most people are constantly learning how to perform new tasks. When presenting a demonstration speech you must consider how to complete your demonstration within the assigned time limits (if given). For example, showing each step completely for a speech on how to make a piñata would likely prove impossible in an 8-10 minute speech as there is significant drying time involved in the process. However, there are ways to present just such a time consuming task. Consider having some steps or stages already completed prior to your speech. In the case of the piñata you could have four versions of piñata one that you will start from scratch, another that has the paper maché dried, and third which has some decorations finished, and then your final product. Using these piñatas, each completed to various stages, would allow you to explain the process to your audience yet not have to literally create a piñata in front of your audience within such a narrow time limit. Similarly, in the case of cooking a dish you could have certain ingredients already mixed, or the dish partially prepared to allow completion in a timely manner. Consider watching a cooking segment on a television show and watch how they are able to prepare a intricate dish in minutes.

Speech of Explanation: This type of speech informs the <u>audience about an abstract or complex idea.</u> For example, you might explain Einstein's theory of relativity, or tell the audience about the geological make-up of Yucca Mountain, or discuss the evolution of your favorite genre music. Notice that while a demonstration speech explains the process this is different than an explanatory speech. For example, the topic of a gun could be configured for either a demonstrative speech discussing how to use a gun or an explanatory speech discussing how a gun works.

Types of Organizational Structures

Once you choose the nature or function of your informative you must consider which type of organization you will use for the body of your speech. While there are several types of organizational structures the four most common are categorical, chronological, sequential and spatial.

Categorical Organization allows for the widest possible variety of structures. Usually the main points do not have any inherent relation to one another and are simply three aspects of the topic. For example, you might explore the Navajo tribe by examining where they lived, what artifacts they are most known for, and famous members of the tribe. Another categorical organization on the same topic might explore traditional foods consumed, changes in the size of the population of the tribe and customary clothing worn.

Chronological Organization puts the main points in order of their occurrence in terms of time. For example you may discuss the civil rights movement in the 1950s, 1960s and 1970s. Another example would be the changes to the Las Vegas Strip over the past decade.

Sequential Organization is used primarily with speeches of <u>demonstration</u>. Sequential order structures main points in terms of their place in a particular process. For example, you may inform the audience on how to make enchiladas by discussing the preparation stage, the cooking stage and the presentation stage.

Spatial Organization allows for the audience to explore a topic based on its physical location and spatial connection. For example, you may talk about the Hawaiian Islands by looking at Kauai, Oahu, Molokai, and Maui.

Many topics could fit into multiple structures but one structure may be a better fit based on the specific focus of your topic. Review the chart below for alternative structures on the topic of the Community College of Southern Nevada (CCSN). Notice the change in thesis and main points.

TOPIC: CCSN

Categorical	Chronological	Sequential	Spatial
Thesis: Interesting aspects of the college.	Thesis: Growth of college since its inception.	Thesis: How to register for classes.	Thesis: Locations of campuses.
Main Points: I. Number of Campuses	Main Points: I. Creation of CCSN in 1971.	Main Points: I. Pick up a schedule of classes	Main Points: I. Cheyenne
II. Popular Classes	II. Growth of CCSN in 1980s	II. Choose desired classes	II. West Charleston
III. Favorite Professors	III. Growth of CCSN in 1990s	III. Use web or phone to register for classes	III. Henderson
	IV. Growth of CCSN in 2000s		IV. Satellite campuses (West Sahara, Green Valley, Summerlin)

Steps in the Preparation of Your Informative Speech

1) **Choose a topic**
   A) Review the section of this textbook on topic selection.
   B) Brainstorm for a topic that you are interested in.
   C) Adapt your topic to your audience.
   D) Narrow the focus of your topic to something that you can handle.

2) **Develop and research for information**
   A) Review the section of this textbook on research.
   B) Write down what you already know about the topic.
   C) Research more on the topic to expand your base of knowledge.
   D) Gather evidence (testimony, statistics, narratives, examples) to support your claims and add substance to your speech.

3) **Organize your material**
   A) Decide on the organizational structure of your speech.
   B) Determine your main points.
   C) Most speeches will have between 3-5 main points.

D) Arrange your main points so that your speech will be fluid and easy to comprehend.

E) Write your introduction and conclusion.

4) **Outline(s)**

A) Prepare a formal outline (review your instructor's specific outline requirements).

B) Prepare a key word or "speaking outline."

C) Write out your note cards (use 3X5 or 4X6 size).

5) **Practice**

A) Practice your speech out loud at least 10 times.

B) Practice your speech with any presentational aids that you may be using.

Sample Informative Speech Topics:

As there is a virtually endless list of potential topics for your informative speech, the best way to develop topics that are of interest to you is to use the brainstorming sheet on the next page. Below is a list of some of the same categories, along with examples of each, to focus your brainstorming.

PEOPLE
Andy Warhol
Ani DiFranco
Barry Bonds
Cesar Chavez
Che' Gueverra
Keith Haring
Kenny Guinn
Louisa May Alcott
Osama bin Laden
Teddy Roosevelt

PLACES
Africa
Australia
Cambodia
Galapagos Islands
Haiti
Hawaii
Iceland
Mars
Massachusetts

ACTIVITES/HOBBIES
Camping
Cars
Computers
Cooking
Dance
Fashion
Home Repair
Investing
Music
Sports

CURRENT EVENTS
Economic Concerns
Education
Environment
Global Concerns
Local Challenges
Pending Laws
Political Races
Race Relations
Social Problems

CULTURAL FESTIVALS
Carnival (Brazil)
Chinese New Year Festival
Cinco de Mayo
Dia de los Muertos (Day of the Dead)
Earth Day
Juneteenth Day (United States)
Kawanza
Maslenitsa (Ukraine)
Perchten (Austria)
Saint Carlo Fair (Italy)

HEALTH/SCIENCE
AIDS
Breast Cancer
Carpel Tunnel Syndrome
Cloning
Homeopathic Medicine
Nano Technology
Obesity
Physical Fitness
Sickle Cell Anemia
Space Travel
Tourettes Syndrome

SAMPLE INFORMATIVE OUTLINE

INTRODUCTION

Attention Material: In the beginning, there was pinball. The game was a huge contraption where you pushed a button on both sides to get the silver ball moving. But back then, you had to go to a bar or pool hall to play pinball. You didn't have the opportunity to play it in your own living room.

Credibility Material: These days, we have Gamecube™, Playstation™ and X-Box™ to purchase at your local department store and play at home with thousands of different games to choose from. So, how did this progression from pinball to videogames occur?

Thesis Statement: Today, I would like to share with you the history of home video games.

Preview: We will look at the evolution of home video games from its origin by first examining the development of video games, next looking at the first game systems. Third, we'll inspect the video game market crash and finally glimpse at the rebirth of the home video game after the crash.

BODY

I. Throughout history, many have contributed to the development of home video games.
  A. The person known to be the forefather or inventor of video games was an engineer called Ralph Baer (Herman, 2000).
    1. In the year of 1949, he was given an assignment to make a television set but Ralph wanted to go beyond than just making a television set (Herman, 2000).
  B. Along with Ralph Baer, other people share in pioneering video games.
    1. In 1958, William Higinbotham was someone who designed an interactive tennis game played on an oscilloscope (Hunter, 2000).
    2. Another, is Steve Russel, in 1961 he programmed a space game on a mainframe computer (Herman, 2000).
    3. And last, Nolan Bushnell who founded Atari in 1972 and launched the video game revolution. (Kent, 2001, xii).

(**Transition**: With a brief history of the pioneers of video games, we can now examine the evolution of home systems and its games.)

II. The earliest of the video game systems have shaped to be what home systems we now play today.
  A. In 1973, the Magnavox Odyssey™ was introduced as the first home video game system (Bios, 2003).
    1. This system did not sell well and only lasted 3 years.
    2. Some of their games were Tennis, Skiing and Simon Says (Bios, 2003).
  B. By the next year, in 1974, Atari Pong™ was released.
    1. Atari Pong™ is recognized as the true first home video game system (Bios, 2003).
    2. It marked the beginning of Atari™ becoming a household name in the US (Bios, 2003).
  C. Besides Atari, there were other home system invented that we're born in the early years of video games.
    1. In 1982, Mattel Electronics released the Intellevision™, a great competitor of Atari™ (Bios, 2003).

2. The arrival of Colecovision™ in 1982 became an even greater competitor with Atari™ (Bios, 2003).

(**Transition**: After the release of the Colecovision™, there was a great video game market crash.)

III. The Video Game Crash started between 1983 & 1984 because of Atari's™ two multimillion dollar disasters.

A. The first disaster came about when Atari 2600™ brought out the version of PAC-MAN (Chance, 1996).

B. After the PAC-MAN loss, Atari™ wanted to recover and signed a contract with Steven Spielberg to create a game based on the movie ET (Chance, 1996).

C. From the two multimillion disasters, everyone lost faith with the video game industry that stores buyers discontinued all video game orders and discounted them to get rid of all the games and systems (Chance, 1996).

(**Transition**: After the crash, it would take two years for the video game industry to rise back to making video games.

IV. The rise and fall of video games in the past has brought upon a new uprising of a series of different video game systems and games to the public for years to come and is still evolving.

A. Among the series of video games is the birth of Nintendo™ which was released in 1986 (Kent, 2001, xiv).

1. The Nintendo Entertainment System was the first 8-bit system on the market after the crash (Bios, 2003).

2. This was the age of the floppy disk, the Commodore 64™, Apple Inc. ™, and the IBM PC™. They didn't think Nintendo™ had a chance and was laughed at. But they were wrong, Nintendo™ skyrocketed (Kent, 2001, 285).

3. One of their great successes was the game Super Mario Brothers. From the internet, Bios said, "Nintendo invented the most successful game in history, "Super Mario Brothers."

4. Nintendo™ released even more new games such as "The Legend of Zelda," "Kid Icarus," and "Punchout."

B. Nintendo™ was not the only system that was released. There were countless others who proved to be great competitors of Nintendo™ which came to a new revolution of video games.

1. Turbografx16 was released in 1989 as the first 16-bit system compared to Nintendo's 8-bit. It put Nintendo™ out of the picture for awhile. But ended fast when Sega Genesis™ comes into the market in that same year (Bios, 2003).

2. Sega Genesis™ became popular with its releases of the John Madden Football Game and Sonic the Hedgehog which started outselling the Super Nintendo Entertainment System (Bios, 2003).

3. Although Nintendo's sales started falling, they rebuild their integrity with their oncoming systems such as N64™ released in 1996 and the now present Gamecube™ with the same revolutionized games of Super Mario & Zelda and even more new games.

4. Today, other systems hold great competitions with Nintendo™, like the Sony Playstation™ with their Final Fantasy series and the new Miscrosoft X-box™ with their best-selling game Halo.

CONCLUSION

Summary Statement: From the pioneers of video games to the making of the Magnavox Odyssey & Atari to its crash and the birth of its new home systems, came a revolution of a multimillion dollar industry that have captivated its followers of all ages through time. On the internet, The Wall Street Journal says, "The battle of the video game industry is coming at a pivotal time in the $9.4 billion domestic industry, whose revenues in 2001 surpassed the U.S. box office for the first time and is still growing."

Concluding Remarks: In the book, The Ultimate History of Video Games, author Steve Baxter, a former producer from the CNN Computer Connection writes, "You can't say that video games grew out of pinball, but you can assume that video games wouldn't have happened without it. It's like bicycles and automobiles. One leads to another and they exist side by side. You had to have bicycles one day to have motor cars" (Kent, 2001, 1).

REFERENCES

Bios, John. "The History of Home Video Games." Reviewpalace.com 13 Aug. 2003 Nintendo64 and Playstation Reviews <http://www.208.46.38.133/reviews/gaminghistory.htm>

Chance, Greg. "The Crash of 1984." Videogames.org 17 Mar. 1996 <http://www.videogames.org/html/crash.html>

Herman, Leonard. "The History of Video Games." Gamespot.com May 2000 CNET Network 1995 <http://www.gamespot.com/gamespot/features/video/hov>

Hunter, William. "From 'Pong' to 'Pac-man'." Designboom.com Sept. 2000 The History of Video Games <http://www.designboom.com/eng/education/pong.html>

Kent, Steven L. The Ultimate History of Video Games: From Pong to Pokemon and Beyond. California: Pima Publishing, 2001

The Wall Street Journal. "Makers of Video Games are Playing Hardball." SouthCoastToday.com 19 May 2002 The Standard Times <http://www.southcoasttoday.com/daily/05-02/05-19-02/d03bu137.htm>

EXERCISE 1 _____

Informative Speech Brainstorming Sheet

People	Places
Issues	**Events**
Activities/Hobbies	**Health/Science**

My topic first choice   _____

My topic second choice   _____

My topic third choice   _____

EXERCISE 2 _____

Research Worksheet

Topic _____

Related terms or "Key words" that you will search for: _____

_____

_____

What references can you use that are located in the Library? _____

_____

_____

List specific references that you have located: _____

1. _____

   _____

2. _____

   _____

3. _____

   _____

4. _____

   _____

5. _____

   _____

What current/recent information on your topic have you located?

_____

_____

_____

Do you have a balanced amount of information for each of your main points?

_____

_____

What information do you still have to locate through other sources (interviews, etc.)?

_____

_____

_____

EXERCISE 3 _____

Outline Worksheet

Your name_____

Topic:
INTRODUCTION
Attention Getter:
Connection with Audience:
Thesis Statement:
Preview:
Transition:

BODY

Main Point I.

Sub-points/Supporting points

Transition:
BODY continued
Main Point II.
Sub-points/Supporting points

Transition:

BODY Continued

Main Point III.

Sub-points/Supporting points

Transition:
CONCLUSION
Summary:
Restate thesis:
Reconnect with audience:
Concluding remarks:
BIBLIOGRAPHY

13 *Persuasive Speaking*

Terms to Know

- Status quo
- Presumption
- Burden of proof
- Prima facie
- Proposition/claim
- Comparative Advantage
- Fallacies
- Proposition of Value
- Tests of Evidence
- Tests of Example
- Stock Issues
- Need
- Inherency
- Solvency
- Motivated Sequence
- Refutation
- Proposition of Fact
- Proposition of Policy
- Tests of Testimony
- Tests of Statistic

Persuasive speaking inherently involves advocating change. However, the type of persuasive speech you are giving is determined by what you are attempting to change and the method by which you go about discussing this change. Do you want to affect tangible change by advocating a shift in legislative or societal policy? Do you want to affect change by encouraging your audience to adopt a different opinion than the one they currently hold and urge them to take immediate action? Do you want to affect change by comparing two opposing positions and suggesting that a choice be made between them? Or do you want to condemn a current course of action by pointing out its flaws? While there are certainly many methods of persuasion, this chapter will answer these questions by focusing on the four most widely used organizational structures: **Stock Issues, Motivated Sequence, Comparative Advantage and Refutation**.

Getting Started

Before you commit to a topic and consequently, an organizational structure, there are some basic definitions regarding the practice of persuasive speaking of which you should be aware. First and foremost, as an advocate of change you are directly challenging the status quo. The **status quo** is simply defined as the current system, prevailing opinion or the existing state of affairs. No matter the method of persuasion you choose, you must realize that you are 'rocking the boat' so to speak. However distasteful the current system might be to some members of your audience, there is often a larger group that feels change is unnecessary and quite frankly, a waste of time. Every persuasive speaker must deal with this reality known as presumption. **Presumption** is simply the belief that most people, most of the time, are comfortable with the way that the status quo is functioning. Subsequently, they hold the belief that the current system should not change unless a good reason is presented for doing so. But be careful here! What determines a 'good' reason is based on a person's value system and core beliefs. What may seem perfectly reasonable and good to you as a speaker may seem insignificant or appalling to some members of your audience. It is important to remember that you cannot and will not persuade every member of your audience. In fact, you may not even affect change in the majority of your audience. However, if you have chosen a topic that is important to you the possibility that you can change even one person's mind should be enough.

So what should persuasive speakers do in order to successfully challenge the status quo and possibly overcome presumption? As an advocate of change, you must shoulder what is known as the burden of proof. The **burden of proof** refers to the speaker's responsibility for creating a solid argument, or one that is supported by evidence and research. It is not enough to merely say something should change, a persuasive speaker must successfully illustrate that change is warranted through the presentation of clear and compelling evidence. To create such a persuasive speech is to create what is known as a prima facie argument. Translated from Latin, **prima facie** simply means 'on its face' or 'at first sight'; not requiring further support to establish credibility or validity. Therefore, a prima facie argument, or case, must meet all of the required structural components of your chosen persuasive organizational pattern. Moreover, such an argument presents enough information to reasonably prove your central or key idea, your **proposition**. Prima facie can also be understood as a set of arguments that are sufficient to overcome presumption. Regardless of the subject matter you eventually choose for your persuasive speech, every persuasive speaker must (1) challenge the status quo, (2) attempt to overcome presumption, (3) shoulder the burden of proof and (4) craft a prima facie argument that satisfies that burden.

Once you have chosen your persuasive topic and perhaps conducted some preliminary research, you must then decide what your central idea will be. As stated above, this central idea, or thesis, is called a **proposition**. A persuasive proposition articulates the subject area of your speech and defines the parameters of your argument. Propositions can be composed around questions of **fact**, **value**, or **policy**.

A proposition of **fact** is a statement that asserts a particular claim to be a certainty. However, for a proposition of fact to work as a persuasive proposition there must be room for argument. Some facts are can be disputed, some cannot. For example, if you wanted to know what team won the 1918 World Series, you would simply look up that information in a sports almanac or reference book. Such a publication would tell you that the Boston Red Sox won the World Series that year. No reasonable person would dispute this fact. As such, this fact would not meet the requirements for a persuasive proposition of fact. Persuasive propositions of fact cannot be answered absolutely. That is, there is no unquestionably correct answer. A true answer does exist, but it is open to interpretation, examination and prediction. For example, a common topic that is often chosen for persuasive speeches is that of capital punishment. A proposition of fact on this topic would assert that something is true about this issue. Such a claim might be: *Capital punishment deters crime*. This statement asserts a factual certainty, but still leaves room for persuasion to occur. No one can know the true answer to the question this topic raises, but many can argue from a wealth of evidence and research that this statement is, in fact, correct. What makes propositions of fact so interesting, however, is that the opposing statement that *Capital punishment does not deter crime* could be presented with just as much speculation and research.

A proposition of **value** is a statement that declares a principle, standard or moral claim. Claims of this nature make a value judgment based on the speakers own sense of what is right or wrong, just or unjust, proper or improper, etc. As such, they can be extremely difficult to prove in the course of a short speech given in the classroom. Because propositions of value are based on a belief system that has most likely taken years to develop, the chances that you will actually be able to alter your audience's sense of morality are quite slim. If you choose to anchor your speech with a proposition of value, you must first define your terms. For example, if you claim that *The death penalty is an ideal form of punishment* you must tell your audience what you mean by "ideal." In other words, what are the standards by which you are evaluating the larger issue of capital punishment? Is it ideal because it prevents recidivism? Because it lessens prison overcrowding? Because it makes the public safer? Once you set these parameters you would then illustrate how your chosen topic, i.e. capital punishment, meets those standards.

A proposition of **policy** is defined as a statement that outlines a specific course of action. This does not mean that speeches that center around propositions of policy do not rely on factual material or value statements. Of course you will use factual material, i.e. evidence, to support your claims. Your personal opinion or value belief regarding your chosen issue will also be obvious to the audience. However, to what end do these factual and value based statements support a specific course of action? That is the question you must answer when developing a speech around a proposition of policy. To advocate specific and tangible change, you must tell the audience what should happen to change the status quo. In fact, a good rule of thumb is to make sure that the word *should* appears in your proposition. Propositions like *Capital punishment should be abolished* and *Capital punishment should be used in every state* both advocate a clear belief (one con, the other pro) and would need to use a variety of supporting material to be credible. However, the phrasing of the proposition is such that the audience knows the speaker is advocating a very specific policy shift in the status quo. In such a speech, not only it is the responsibility of the speaker to show that change is necessary, he or she must also present clear solutions that would allow for this proposed change to take place.

Organizing your Speech

Stock Issues

A **Stock Issues** persuasive structure simply refers to the major points that must be addressed in your speech. There are three stock issues that must be addressed and so this structure works best with a speech that contains three main points. In order to strengthen your stock issues speech it is also a good idea to include specific sub-points that further define your position.

I. **Need/Problem**: Here you show your audience that there is a need for change by illustrating the problems that currently exist in the status quo. You should address the *nature* (sub-point A) of the problem as well as its *extent* (sub-point B). The nature of the problem gives the audience a basic definition or description of the problem while the extent illustrates how widespread the problem is or how it is affecting people.

II. **Inherency/Cause**: Here you show your audience how the status quo is failing to address its problems or how the status quo is perpetuating the problems. Outline causality by illustrating how cause is both an *institutional* (sub-point A) and *individual* (sub-point B) issue. Institutional refers to how society, government, or media cause the problem while individual refers to how we, as members of your audience, allow the problem to continue.

III. Solvency/Solutions: Here you present clear suggestions for change. You should argue for specific solutions here, not vague ideas. Just as you addressed institutional and individual causality in your second point, you want to present both *institutional* (sub-point A) and *individual* (sub-point B) solutions here. Institutional solutions need to tell your audience what society needs to do to change. Should new laws be passed? Should funding for certain programs increase? Should penalties be applied to those who do not comply? Tell your audience as precisely as you can what solutions need to take place. Individual solutions must involve your audience. What can we do to facilitate change? Should be contact our congressional representatives? Should we volunteer and donate either time or money? Should we simply 'get the word out' and share what we have learned? No matter what you think we need to do to change the status quo, it is important that you give us specific recommendations.

Below is an example of an outline that follows the Stock Issues format for persuasive speaking.

SAMPLE PERSUASIVE SPEECH OULINE

INTRODUCTION

Attention-Getter/Statement of Topic/Link to Audience: Children are our future. We hear this everywhere. But are we doing enough to protect our future? My topic is sports coaches and officials in private organizations. If you are a parent, sister or brother or know a child this should be an important topic to you, because our children are being victimized and we are allowing it.

Thesis: Fingerprinting and background checks should be mandatory for all people who coach and officiate children in youth sports.

Preview: I will tell you about some of the problems, causes, and solutions surrounding this issue.

Transition: To begin with I will tell you about the problem and its extent.

BODY

I. Problem: Coaches and Officials are abusing our children.
  A. Nature: Pedophiles are becoming coaches.
   1. Coaches are molesting children. "It [child molestation] occurs with enough regularity across the country, at all levels [of society], that it should be viewed as a public health problem." (Nack, William, and Yaeger, Don. "Every Parent's Nightmare." <u>Sports Illustrated</u> 13 Sept. 1999: 42-53.)
   2. Pedophiles can be friendly, helpful, and manipulative because they blend in and this is what makes them so dangerous. (Johnson, Becca Cowan, and For Kids Sake, Inc. <u>For Their Sake Recognizing, Responding to, and Reporting Child Abuse</u>. Martinsville: American Camping Association, 1992.)
  B. Extent: The extent of the problem can be found in the numbers of children at risk and the news reports of molested children.
   1. There are approximately forty-two million children involved in privately run organized sports each year that could potentially be at risk. (United States. US Census Bureau, National Data Book. <u>Statistical Abstract of the United States</u>. Washington: US Department of Commerce, 1999.)

2. We can find this occurring in our own backyard. "A Las Vegas baseball coach who molested seven young boys will likely spend the rest of his life in prison following his conviction. The majority of the boys Pearson molested were on his baseball team." (Puit, Glenn. "Little League Coach Convicted." <u>Las Vegas Review Journal</u> 29 March 2001: 1A+.)

Transition: Now lets discuss some causes of this problem.

II. Cause: There are several factors that contribute to the problem both by the organizations and the individual parents or guardians.

  A. Institutional: There are no protections in place to stop pedophiles from becoming coaches.

    1. Looking in the Nevada Revised Statutes won't help this problem. "There are no laws mandating fingerprinting and background checks for coaches in private organizations. (Marshall, Richard. Nye County Sheriff's Office. Personal interview. 17, April 2001).

    2. Insurance carriers are concerned about the liability and the lawsuits that may arise with mandatory background and fingerprint checks. (Winton, Richard. "Insurer Warns West Covina on Screening Coaches." <u>Los Angeles Times</u> 18 May 2000: B1.)

  B. Individual: There is a lack of adults willing or able to volunteer their time.

    1. We are giving authority, over our children, to strangers we know nothing about. "Parents today are so busy, they're allowing coaches to take over the after school hours, and that's the foot in the door pedophiles need." (Nack, William, and Yaeger, Don. "Every Parent's Nightmare." <u>Sports Illustrated</u> 13 Sept. 1999: 42-53.)

    2. The checks and balances to deter pedophiles are not in place because some leagues need coaches. "Some leagues don't want to discourage scarce volunteers." (Hendrick, Bill. "Who's Coaching our Kids Leagues: Taking a Closer Look." <u>The Atlanta Constitution</u> 09 March 2001: A1. Online. <u>Electric Library.</u> 27 Mar. 2001.)

Transition: While these numbers and examples are terrible, the majority of coaches and officials are not out to hurt our children; however we must make the safety of our children number one and protect them against those that are.

III. Solution: To solve this problem we need both legislature and parental involvement.

  A. Institutional: We must create laws mandating fingerprinting and background checks for coaches and officials in private organizations.

    1. Organizations that do not do fingerprinting and background checks would face criminal charges with fines up to $2,000.00 and possibly jail penalties up to 2 years in county jail.

    2. The federal government should create a national Coach's Card where coaches and officials are registered which would create a way to track and have accountability for coaches and officials.

  B. Individual: We need to be accountable for the safety of our children.

    1. We must meet and get to know the coaches and officials that are involved with our children.

    2. We can form networks with other parents we know to help watch out for our children, so our children are never alone with a single adult.

    3. We must talk to our children about abuse and pay attention to any changes in them.

    4. We need to get involved with the organizations that our children are involved with.

CONCLUSION

Summary: I have discussed some of the problems, causes and solutions associated with coaches and officials in private organizations hurting our children.

Restate Thesis: Fingerprinting and background checks should be mandatory for all people who coach and officiate children in youth sports.

Reconnect with Audience/Concluding Remarks: In closing I would like to leave you with one final example. A man, who was molested by his coach 20 years earlier, hired a private detective to find that coach. The detective found out this man had been convicted two times of child molestation, but was still coaching in the West Coast's Little League capital, San Bernadino, CA. This man had been a "winning" coach and umpiring for the Little League organization for 6 years. The detective advised a board member they had a convicted child molester as a coach. Given this coach's winning record, the board still voted to keep him and ousted the board member that brought the information to them. One board member even asked the coach if he needed a lawyer to defend his reputation. Shortly after this board decision a boy came forward and the coach was arrested and convicted for 39 counts of child molestation involving 5 children that dated back almost five years. This "winning" coach will spend the rest of this life in prison. Children are our future we must protect them.

EXERCISE 1: See if you can fit your topic into this stock issues format.

Your persuasive speech topic: _____

Problem: _____

_____

_____

_____

Cause: _____

_____

_____

_____

Solution: _____

_____

_____

_____

Motivated Sequence

The **motivated sequence** persuasive structure is similar to stock issues in that it works well for speeches that are demanding immediate action. The sequence has five steps:

I. **Attention:** This is exactly what you have been doing in your previous speeches. You can do this by relating to the audience, arousing curiosity, presenting a startling quotation or statistic, or posing a specific question.

II. **Need:** This is virtually the same point as was presented in the discussion regarding stock issues. Here you must illustrate a need for change by pointing out flaws in the status quo to your audience. You must show that a problem (or many problems) exists and support your claims with statistics, examples and testimony. You also need to relate this problem to your audience. Make them care about this issues. Show them why it should concern them.

III. **Satisfaction:** Now that you have aroused the interest of your audience and clearly shown how they are affected by the problems in the status quo, you must present a way to fix the problem. You should present a specific plan and show how it will solve the harms in the current system. Be sure to be specific here. Your audience will want to know exactly what your plan entails and how it will work.

IV. **Visualization:** Here you need to discuss the benefits that would emerge once your solution has been adopted. Help your audience "visualize" the positive outcomes of your solution. You can also view this step as a place to present the advantages that your plan would bring to the status quo. Show your audience how society becomes better once your plan is adopted.

V. **Action:** This step is a specific plan for how your audience can help make your proposed solution a reality. Identify exactly what you want your listeners to do. You have already outlined a plan of action, now tell your audience what their role should be in enacting it.

Below is an example of a rough draft outline that follows the Motivated Sequence format for persuasive speaking. Before you would give this speech, you would, of course, find suitable evidence to support your claims.

Example: Immunization of Children

Attention: 15% of Las Vegas children ages 2-5 years old have not been immunized.

Need: Many new parents do not know where or when to get their children immunized. This lack of knowledge is causing illness and even death in cases where it could have been prevented.

Solution: We must seek to inform new parents about getting their kids immunized—a free option to all people in Las Vegas.

Visualization: Diseases like Small pox, Measles, Mumps, rubella and more can be deadly for anyone, especially children. All of these diseases can be completely prevented by getting your children immunized.

Action: If you are a parent, or plan on being one, make sure you have your children immunized. We must also write our congressional representatives to urge for more funding to increase community education about this life or death issue.

EXERCISE 2: See if you can fit your topic into this motivated sequence format.

Your Persuasive speech Topic: _____

Attention: _____

_____

Need: _____

_____

_____

Satisfaction: _____

_____

_____

_____

Visualization: _____

_____

_____

_____

Action: _____

_____

_____

_____

Comparative Advantage

The **comparative advantage** organizational structure is used to compare two alternatives. Sometimes this design is referred to as Pro/Con organization. This type of structure is ideal when your audience is already aware that a problem exists. Given this reality, you would not need to spend time determining that a problem exists; rather, you can discuss the advantages and disadvantages of competing solutions. The best way to do this is to organize your speech around three main points composed of the following:

I. **Pro Side:** This main point would discuss and support a proposed solution to a widely understood problem. You would tell the audience why the proposed solution could be seen as a good idea.

II. **Con Side:** This main point would discuss the disadvantages associated with the above solution. As a speaker, you are trying to make sure that the audience understands the harm that can come from implementing the proposed solution.

III. **Position/Reason:** In this point you must take a stance, either pro or con. Your previous points have presented both sides of the issues, now it is time to commit to a course of action and clearly explain your reasons for doing so. Here you should also try to convince the audience that your position is the best one and should be adopted by them.

Below is an example of a rough draft outline that follows the Comparative Advantage format for persuasive speaking. Before you would give this speech, you would, of course, find suitable evidence to support your claims.

Example: Yucca mountain project

Pro Side: If we develop Yucca mountain as a disposal site for nuclear waste then this new industry will create many more jobs for Nevada citizens. Scientists contend that Yucca mountain is theoretically the best place to develop this waste cite.

Con Side: The plan is unsafe because it has never actually been done. Yucca Mountain is on a fault line so there is a risk of damage due to an earthquake. There is a risk of further harm because of the unsafe manner of transportation of toxic nuclear waste.

<u>Your position and reasons (either pro/con)</u>: While the Yucca Mountain project would offer new jobs, the economic boost would come at a real threat to public safety. There are too many unknown factors so we should NOT go forth with this project. We should attempt to develop other methods of nuclear waste disposal instead.

EXERCISE 3: See if you can fit your topic into this comparative advantage format.

Your Persuasive speech Topic: _____

Pro side: _____

_____

_____

_____

Con side: _____

_____

_____

_____

Present the reasons for your position (either pro/con): _____

_____

_____

_____

Refutation

This **refutation** pattern of persuasive organization involves a systematic negation of a particular argument. In a well-organized format, the speaker attempts to persuade the audience by disproving the opposing position while simultaneously supporting his or her own. This pattern tends to work best when you know that your audience already disagrees with you. You would then begin by acknowledging common and popular arguments about your chosen topic, expose the logical flaws in that type of reasoning and present counter-arguments (i.e. your position) that are supported by a variety of supporting material and evidence. While there are many strategies for organizing a persuasive speech of refutation, the following structure is an excellent and introductory way to organize your main points. Keep in mind that this four step process should be used to develop each main point, however many you decide there should be.

I. **First main point: Identify the point to be refuted.** To make a speech of refutation work, you must first set the stage for your audience. What position or common belief are you opposing? The more specific you can be, the easier it will be for your audience to follow the chain of your argument.

   A. **Subpoint: Label and signpost your refutation.** This step requires you to clearly and succinctly state your position. This is not the time to elaborate, but merely to make a specific claim about the opposing position. Here you are trying to label the opposition to frame your specifics arguments that will follow.

   B. **Subpoint: Support your claims.** Now that you have identified the position you are opposing as well as briefly outlined your response to it, it is time to develop your argument. What is your reasoning? What supporting material or evidence do you have that supports your position?

C. Subpoint: Show the impact of your argument. Here you need to show the significance of the arguments you have just made. It is your responsibility to guide the audience toward your analysis of your chosen issue. Do not assume that they will automatically see things your way. It is the speaker's responsibility to direct the audience.

Again, these four steps should be repeated for every main point of your speech. Also remember that a refutation speech is no different than any other speech in that it still needs a clear introduction and conclusion to complete it. Below is an example of one rough draft main point that follows the Refutation format for persuasive speaking. Before you would give this speech, you would, of course, find suitable evidence to support your claims, develop more than one main point, and create a suitable introduction and conclusion.

Example: Euthanasia and Physician-Assisted Suicide

I. First main point: Many people believe that euthanasia will be used to kill a sick patient against their own will and consequently, do not support legislation supporting it.

   A. Subpoint: This argument is based on the irrational fear that one day you may be ill and others will make the choice to die for you.

   B. Subpoint: Although these beliefs may seem grounded in reality, in places where euthanasia is legal (like Oregon) it is tightly regulated.(explain in detail the regulations in place in Oregon and elsewhere)

   C. Subpoint: When one looks at the strong evidence regarding the regulation and control of legalized euthanasia, it becomes clear that the possibility of being put to death against your will simply does not happen in places where strict legislation is in place.

EXERCISE 4: See if you can develop a main point to fit into this refutation format.

Your Persuasive speech Topic: _____

Main point: _____

_____

_____

_____

Subpoint: _____

_____

_____

Subpoint: _____

_____

_____

Subpoint: _____

_____

_____

Persuasive Topic Suggestions

Now that you have been presented with several persuasive strategies, it is time (if you haven't already done so) to start thinking about a topic. Try to approach your persuasive speaking assignment with passion. What issues do you care about? If you had the power to change something in the status quo what would it be? Ask yourself: What *should* change? Below is a list of suggested topics, but remember, this list is just a proposal. Feel free to choose a topic on your own.

1. marijuana legalization
2. nuclear waste disposal
3. lowering the drunk driving standard
4. smoking in public places
5. internet regulation
6. school dress codes
7. handgun control
8. family counseling services
9. welfare reform
10. sports betting
11. sex education in schools
12. animal experimentation
13. road rage
14. free music on the internet
15. ritalin
16. cloning
17. tax reform
18. driving license availability
19. global warming
20. cell phone use
21. dental hygiene
22. drug testing
23. health care reform
24. organic produce
25. prison rehabilitation programs
26. euthanasia
27. teen pregnancy
28. mandatory newborn screening
29. capital punishment and racial discrimination
30. bilingual education

Once you have decided on a topic you should move on to the brainstorming sheet that follows. Use the available spaces to elaborate on your topic idea and to frame larger issues that you can begin to research.

Persuasive Speech Brainstorming Sheet

College Issues	Local Issues

State Issues	National Issues

Global Issues	Home (Family) Issues

My topic first choice _____

My topic second choice _____

My topic third choice _____

Now that you have chosen a topic and begun to brainstorm on how you may want to develop it, it is time to start conducting research. Use the sheet below to gather preliminary evidence and supporting material.

Persuasive Research Worksheet

Topic _____

Related terms or "Key words" that you will search for: _____

_____

_____

What references can you use that are located in the Library? _____

_____

_____

List specific references that you have located:_____

    1. _____

       _____

    2. _____

       _____

    3. _____

       _____

    4. _____

       _____

    5. _____

       _____

What current/recent information on your topic have you located?

_____

_____

_____

Do you have a balanced amount of information for each of your main points?

_____

_____

What information do you still have to locate through other sources (interviews, etc.)?

_____

_____

_____

_____

Troubleshooting

Before you begin to construct an outline for your persuasive speech (however rough it may be) there are certain concerns that must be addressed; namely, avoiding fallacious reasoning and choosing credible evidence. **Fallacies** are inconsistencies or breaks in logical argument. Although they can be very effective (just consider television advertisements) they are unethical methods of persuasion and should be avoided. Even if the speaker does not intend to willingly deceive his or her audience, fallacies can sometimes slip into a speech simply because at first glance they seem reasonable. By knowing what fallacies are and more importantly, how they work, you can hopefully avoid including them in your speech. Below are some of the most widely used fallacies. This list is by no means comprehensive, but merely contains some of the most common illogical and thus, fallacious, reasoning you are likely to hear.

Common Fallacies

1. **Generalization:** (Hasty Generalization) An inadequate number of examples to warrant the claim.

   Example: The newspapers are full of nothing but sex and crime. In last night's paper, for instance, there were five sex and crime stories on page one.

2. **Sign:** (Insufficient Sign) An inadequate number of indicants to warrant the claim.

   Example: John's crazy. I saw him talking to himself.

   Guilt by Association: An indictment of a person or issue by noting the characteristics of a group or program with which he, she, or it is associated.

   Example: You can't support that plan. The National Rifle Association supports it.

3. **Cause:** (Mistaken Cause) A claim that a partial cause is entirely responsible for something.

   Example: GM had a bad trade year. The U.S. had a bad trade year. GM's bad year caused the U.S. trade deficit.

   Post Hoc Ergo Propter Hoc: (After this, therefore, because of this). A claim that mistakes sequentiality for causality.

   Example: I went to speech class and then got into an accident. Therefore, speech class caused me to get into an accident.

4. **Analogy:** (False Analogy) An unwarranted comparison in which you are comparing things that are not at all alike.

   Example: We shouldn't criticize and punish human beings for their actions. Are we angry with the stone falling and the flame rising?

5. **Authority:** (Appeal to Authority) A belief that citing an authority decides an argument or citing testimony outside of the authority's field of competence.

   Example: A doctor said it so it must be true!

   Example: Your art teacher said Einstein was wrong about relativity and you should believe him because he is your teacher.

6. **Principle:** Applying a general statement to which it cannot and was not intended to be applied.

   Example: No one is ever justified in taking away someone else's property. Therefore, the federal government cannot legally collect taxes.

7. **Shifting the Burden of Proof:** Arguing that the opponent must disprove your claim.

Example: Lowering the legal level of intoxication while driving will lower accidents. Prove that it won't!

8. **Irrelevant Reason:** Arguing a reason that is irrelevant to the claim.

Examples follow:

> **Appeal to Majority:** (Ad Populum) Arguing that an idea is true because the majority believes it to be true.
>
> Example: Soccer is the best sport because it is the most popular worldwide.
>
> **Appeal to Pity:** (Ad Misercordiam) An argument that appeals to an audience's sense of pity.
>
> Example: I've got to get an A in this class. I'm a nursing major.
>
> **Appeal to Fear:** (Ad Baculum) An argument that uses the threat of harm.
>
> Example: You should tell me the information I need or I will kill you.
>
> **Appeal Against the Person:** (Ad Hominem) An argument that attacks a person's views by abusing their personality, beliefs, etc., instead of indicating the error of the argument.
>
> Example: You can't believe anything he says, he's an atheist.
>
> **You're Another:** (Tu Quoque) An argument that present a counter-charge that your opponent (or someone else) is guilty, too.
>
> Example: Why should I quit smoking? You smoke more than I do!

9. **False Dichotomy:** An argument that invalidly divides the world into two parts.

Example: You are either with us or you are against us.

10. **Slippery Slope:** Arguing that one action will inevitably lead to similar, but less desirable actions.

Example: Let the state register handguns and the next thing you know, they'll ban them.

11. **Fallacy of Qualifier:** An argument that neglects to identify its criteria for evaluation or fails to qualify its claim.

Example: You're going to fail the exam. After all, you only studied for an hour and a half.

Avoiding fallacies when creating a good persuasive speech is only half the battle. You must also bolster your claims with solid evidence and supporting material. Although you have already been presented with methods of conducting ethical and responsible research in a previous chapter, given that persuasive speaking requires you to attempt to change the attitudes, beliefs and even the behavior of your audience it is worthwhile to revisit this topic. Whenever you use supporting material in your speech, you must try to select the most credible and ethical evidence possible. Below are several guidelines that help you choose good supporting material whether it is testimony, examples, or statistics.

Tests of Evidence

Tests of Testimony

1. Source Identification: Is the source of the testimony identified?
2. Source Ability: Is the source of the data competent to report or interpret the situation in this field?
3. Source Willingness: It the source willing to report or interpret the situation fairly?

4. Verifiability: Is the source available to all?

5. Recency: Has anything changed from the date of the testimony?

6. Context: Is the testimony used in a manner consistent with the meaning and intent of the source?

7. Internal Consistency: Is the testimony consistent with other evidence from the same source?

8. External Consistency: Is the testimony consistent with other evidence from unrelated sources?

Tests of Examples

1. Typicality: Are the instances or examples typical?

2. Sufficiency: Are there a sufficient number of instances or examples to prove your point?

3. Accountability: Are negative instances accounted for? In other words, how do you explain examples contrary to your argument?

Tests of Statistics

1. Inadequately Defined Terms: Are the terms of the categories clearly defined?

2. Unknowable Statistics: Are the statistics knowable?
   a. Barrier to data collection: Is it possible to count the data?
   b. Inadequate reporting of data: Are all cases reported?
   c. Uncritical Projection of Trends: Is a trend predicted without consideration for future changes?
   d. Quality of Estimate: Does the source of the statistic meet relevant source tests?

3. Illegitimate Use of Averages: Are the three types of averages used appropriately?
   a. Mean: Arithmetic average
   b. Median: Middle score
   c. Mode: Most frequent

4. Abuse of Percentages: Are percentages used correctly?
   a. Carelessness: Do the percentages exceed 100%?
   b. Failure to Specify the Base: Is the base of the percentage indicated?
      1. Unusual base: Does the size of the base mislead?
      2. Confusion with Numerical Data: Are the percentages inappropriately treated as numerical data, i.e. added or subtracted?

5. Abuse of Inferential Statistics
   a. Biased Sampling: Is a representative sample utilized?
   b. Biased Questioning: Are the questions constructed fairly?

Tips for Persuasive Speaking

Now that you have been presented with a variety of persuasive organizational structures as well as methods for developing and supporting your argument, it is time to mention a few tips regarding the presentation and delivery of your speech. The following is a list of guidelines to consider before practicing and ultimately presenting your speech.

- Make sure your solutions directly address the problem. Stay focused and don't deal with issues beyond the scope of the problem.
- Consider using presentational aids. Presentational aids, when used effectively make your arguments clearer.
- Offer your audience clear and specific steps they can follow to resolve the problem.
- Consider addressing any opposing arguments. Don't ignore opposing arguments to your solution, answer them and you will strengthen your arguments.
- Enhance your credibility. Cite information and evidence from credible sources to strengthen your arguments. (Ethos)
- Use emotional appeals to get audiences involved and motivated by your arguments. (Pathos)
- Use logical arguments to help your audience rationally understand key elements of your issue. (Logos)
- Remember, most persuasive speeches that you give in the classroom are not value speeches. Do not be judgmental or self-righteous in either your approach to your topic or in your language choices.
- Prepare yourself to answer questions your audience might have after your speech is over. In many instances your instructor will allow a question and answer period to take place immediately following your presentation. Do not be defensive or take opposing questions personally. In most instances your audience will just want to clarify information. If an audience member does overtly disagree with you, take their comments in stride. Remember, you cannot persuade everyone. Keep your cool and learn to defend your position rationally.

EXERCISES

1) Refer back to the suggested list of persuasive topics listed in this chapter. Choose a topic that interests you and write three propositions regarding that topic. Be sure to write a proposition of fact, a proposition of value and a proposition of policy.

2) Listed below are several statements of fallacies. Referring back to the fallacy definitions listed in this chapter, identify the fallacy that you most clearly think is at work. Choose only one fallacy for each statement and do not repeat your answers. Also be as precise as you can. For example, if you think a statement illustrates a type of irrelevant reason, identify specifically which type of irrelevant reason is present.

Fallacy Identification Exercise

1. "I'm a pepper, he's a pepper, we're all peppers. Wouldn't you like to be a pepper, too?"

2. I had a bad experience getting my first haircut. I had a bad experience getting my second haircut. I'm never getting my hair cut again. It's bound to be a bad experience.

3. Peter is in a lot of trouble. Peter laughed in church and we all know it's wrong to laugh in church.

4. You'd better identify these fallacies correctly or I'll know that you haven't been paying attention in class.

5. How can you oppose the war in Iraq? Donald Rumsfield supports it and he's the Secretary of Defense.

6. It you let that activist group march in Washington, D. C., the next thing you know they'll want to march down the Strip.

7. President Truman's proposal typifies the thinking of this little, little man.

8. After using Crest's whitening toothpaste, Zach got an "A" on his speech. I bet if I use Crest's whitening toothpaste I'll get an "A" too.

9. This test shouldn't count because there are too many assignments due at this point in the semester, and I'm tired, and my parents will kill me if I don't get an "A."

10. Why did I lose points for going overtime in my speech? April was overtime, too!

3) Listed below are several hypothetical pieces of evidence. The following list of hypothetical pieces of evidence violates a variety of tests of evidence. Referring back to the Tests of Evidence listed in this chapter, identify as many errors as you can spot. Remember, identify the type of evidence first then identify what is wrong with it. In other words, if you identify a piece of evidence as testimony then look in the tests of testimony section to find your answer.

Tests of Evidence Exercise

1. Two well-known political analysts, Evans and Novak, predicted that Sander Levin, the Republican nominee, would lose the up coming Michigan gubernatorial election. They cited a poll of 64 blue-collar workers from the capital city to bolster their argument. The poll showed 36% for Levin, 42% for Levin's opponent, and 22% undecided.

2. In recent Senate debates, some senators cited the corrupt labor practices of the Teamster's union as justification for legislation regulating all labor unions in the United States.

3. Last month, U. S. purchases of foreign goods increased only 25% while U. S. exports increased 50%. The U. S. trade deficit is only half as bad as it used to be.

4. According to the American Tobacco Institute, there is no concrete evidence demonstrating a causal relationship between smoking and lung cancer.

5. A popular journalist recently wrote an article in which he claimed to know "what's really going on inside the White House." He reported that he had spent a week visiting Washington D.C. and had the inside scoop.

6. The average age of students in this class is 22.

4) With important troubleshooting tools behind you, you can now begin to outline your persuasive speech. Use the following worksheet to tentatively organize your persuasive speech.

Persuasive Outline Worksheet

Your name_____

Topic:
INTRODUCTION
Attention Getter:
Connection with Audience:
Thesis Statement:
Preview:
Transition:

BODY

Main Point I.

Sub-points/Supporting points

Transition:

BODY continued

Main Point II.

Sub-points/Supporting points

.

Transition:
BODY Continued
Main Point III.
Sub-points/Supporting points

Transition:

CONCLUSION

Summary:

Restate thesis:

Reconnect with audience:

Concluding remarks:

BIBLIOGRAPHY

14 *Impromptu Speaking*

Terms to Know

- Impromptu delivery
- Key-word note card
- Impromptu grab bag
- Prep time
- Impromptu theme
- Impromptu quotation

Probably the most common speech you will ever have to give is an impromptu speech. Once you leave the artificial speaking environment of the classroom, this type of speaking is most often what you will encounter both in the workplace and in a myriad of social situations. When a boss or supervisor asks you to offer an opinion regarding a specific project or asks you to make a brief presentation outlining the important points of a meeting, you are giving an impromptu speech. When a good friend asks you to make a toast without prior preparation or asks you to say a few words at a dinner, you are giving an impromptu speech.

An impromptu speech is a presentation given with very little time for preparation. This kind of speaking is known as speaking "off the top of your head," "off the cuff" or "from the hip." However, many people make the mistake of believing that impromptu speaking means the speaker is "just making stuff up." While it is true that the speaker lacks adequate time to research or even develop his or her remarks, this does not and should not translate into the speaker fabricating material. Being a good impromptu speaker does not mean you are "B.S.-ing" your way through your presentation. On the contrary, being a good impromptu speaker means that you have learned to organize your thoughts quickly and clearly. It is the purpose of this brief chapter to present you with the specific tools you need to develop this skill.

For your impromptu speech in this class you will be given a specific amount of time (usually a few minutes) to prepare a speech on a topic you have either chosen or that your instructor has assigned to you. You will usually receive your topic 2-3 minutes before you are expected to speak. This 2-3 minute time in which you plan your speech is known as your **prep time**. Despite what you may think, prep time is not a time for panic. If you keep yourself calm and collected, this time can be more than adequate to develop a short presentation. During your valuable prep time you should put your ideas down on a note card in key-word format. This **key-word note card** will guide you through your speech. Please refer back to the organization chapter for tips on creating a key-word outline.

Although each instructor is different, you can usually expect an impromptu speech to last anywhere from 2-4 minutes. While each instructor has a different format you will likely be given a set of topics, questions, quotations or issues from which you must select. While you only have a limited amount of time to prepare there are steps you can take to use your time efficiently.

For the sake of example, let's assume you have been given two minutes of prep time. How should you divide your time?

1. **Topic Selection:** First and foremost, if your instructor has given you several topics from which to choose, you must choose one quickly. Prep time should not be squandered on topic selection. Make your decision as fast as you can and do not change your mind.

2. **Define your Topic:** The second thing you should do is try to identify a main idea connected to your chosen topic. In a sense, you are trying to develop a kernel of thought from which to build a thesis. For most impromptu topics this means you are defining your chosen subject. Try asking yourself this question: What does this topic mean to me?

3. **Take a Position:** Next you should take a position regarding your topic. Do you agree or disagree with its definition? Is the main idea of your topic a good thing or a bad thing? This step, combined with step two, composes your thesis statement. In other words, to develop a quick thesis statement for an impromptu speech, first you define your topic and then you take a position.

4. **Brainstorm:** Generate a quick list of everything you can think of that can be connected to your topic. Think of past experiences you have had, stories friends have shared with you, books you have read, movies you have seen, etc. From this list you will choose what will become your main points. Give each main idea a clear and concise label that you can use in your preview.

At this point in your prep time you should have used 30-45 seconds.

5. **Organize:** Look at the three labels you have given to your main points. Decide in what order you want to present them in your speech. What should the first point be? The second? The third? Once you have determined the order of points take time to develop each one. Try to include *specific* examples. The more specific you can be, the stronger your argument and the longer your speech will be.

At this point in your prep time you should have used 1 1/2 minutes.

6. **Introduction and Conclusion:** Develop your opening and closing. Don't forget to include a preview and summary of your main points in your speech. This will help your audience follow along and will help you stay on track.

**At this point you should have used 2 minutes and will begin your speech.
The basic format you should have created looks like this:**

Impromptu Outline

Introduction
Attention device
Statement of topic
Definition of topic
Position
Preview: I.
             II.
             III.

Body
I.   Main point
     -Specific examples
II. Main point
     -Specific examples
III. Main point
     -Specific examples

Conclusion
Summary
Restatement of topic, definition and position
Concluding remarks

When delivering your speech, remember that no one in your audience expects you to deliver an impromptu speech flawlessly. **Impromptu delivery** is, by definition, delivery with no time for practice. When you stumble over words or take a few seconds to collect your thoughts, it is okay! Try your best to be confident and don't worry about errors in delivery. That said, also remember that the more structured you are, the easier it will be to appear confident about your speech. A good tip for success is to write the basic outline above on your note card *before* you come to class and *before* you choose your topic. With the skeletal outline in place before you start your prep time, you are in a much better position to simply fill in the blanks as you think of them. Doing this also ensures that you will not forget an important component of structure during prep time when you may be somewhat distracted.

Types of Impromptu Topics

Impromptu topics can be as varied as the speaking environments in which you may find yourself. However, within the classroom setting impromptu topics can usually be group into several categories. If you instructor elects to choose something different, you can still follow the basic approach to impromptu speaking outlined here to organize your thoughts.

Impromptu Themes

Impromptu themes are usually just one word abstracts. This means that they consist of simply one word that lacks a concrete and tangible definition. Examples of one word abstracts that you may encounter in the classroom are words like *justice, love, opportunity, etc.* If you find yourself confronted with this type of topic, you can relax a bit. Most of the hard work has already been done. Instead of trying to decide what the topic is all about, you just need to determine what the word means to you. You are not trying to duplicate the dictionary definition, but rather, telling us how you define the word. For example, if you chose the word *justice* as your topic, you could perhaps argue that justice can be defined as fairness to everyone in all circumstances. Not everyone in your audience may like your definition or even agree with it, but you can explain yourself and support this position with the development of your main points. You can also clarify your definition when you state your position. Saying something like "I think justice can be defined as fairness to everyone in all circumstances which is a good thing that society should try to achieve" includes both your definition and position as firmly advocates your thesis.

Impromptu Quotations

Impromptu quotations are statements attributed to others that contain an observation about human behavior. Topics of this nature on the surface seem more complicated than one word abstracts, but at their core they are virtually the same. If given these types of topics, you must first determine what truth about human behavior they are trying to illustrate. Once you have done that, you are essentially at the same starting point as one word abstracts and can thus, follow the same steps as outlined above. The key is to first determine what one word abstract is embedded in the quotation. Consider the following example:

Adversity makes men think of God

What does this quotation mean to you? The first step to constructing a good impromptu speech is to answer this question. One answer might be that individuals who are not particularly religious turn to the idea of God when their lives become difficult. One could then make the argument that this quotation speaks of the hypocrisy inherent in this behavior. Again, your audience may or may not agree with your interpretation of this quotation, but it is your job as a speaker to state a clear definition and position and support it with several main points.

Impromptu Grab Bag

Impromptu grab bag consists of choosing a physical, tangible object out of a bag. The object you choose is the topic for your speech. Just like a one word abstract or a quotation, an object impromptu must begin with your definition of what your chosen object means to you. Once you have decided on a definition then your speech will proceed in the same fashion as described above. For example, if your instructor chooses this method for assigning impromptu speech topics, you may end up choosing something like a magnifying glass, paper clip or computer disk.

If you chose one of these topics how would you define it? Perhaps a magnifying glass could be defined as a symbol of introspection or self-examination. A paper clip could be seen as the human need to organize and hold things together. A computer disk could represent our reliance on technology or the importance of scientific progress. Remember, any way that you choose to define the object is fine, as long as you take a position and support your definition with main points and specific examples.

Now that you understand the basic dynamics of impromptu speaking, use the following examples to practice the various approaches you may be required to take for this kind of speech.

EXERCISES

1. Choose one of the three quotations below and develop an impromptu outline for your chosen topic. If possible, have a classmate time you so that you only use two minutes of prep time.
   a. Absence makes the heart grow fonder.
   b. The only thing some people ever do is grow old.
   c. To rebel in season is not to rebel.

2. Choose one of the three impromptu themes below and develop an impromptu outline for your chosen topic. If possible, have a classmate time you so that you only use two minutes of prep time.
   a. Luck
   b. Adversity
   c. Honor

3. Have a classmate choose an object they have with them for your impromptu topic. Create and impromptu outline for this topic as if you were going to give the speech. If possible, have this same classmate time you so that you only use two minutes of prep time.

4. When you have completed your impromptu speech, consider filling out the following self-evaluation. Doing so will help you monitor your growth as a speaker.

Impromptu Self-Evaluation

Content:
How has the substance of my speaking changed?
Have I met the assignment requirements?
Am I adequately explaining and supporting my ideas?

Organization:
Are my speeches clearly organized?
Did I complete all of the required components of a speech? (Introduction, Body, Conclusion)

Delivery:
Has my delivery improved? How? (Explore each of the key areas)

Preparation:
Was I adequately prepared to give the speech?
Did I use my prep time wisely?

Strengths:
What was my great strength?

Weakness:
What area(s) do I need most to improve?
How can I work on improving this aspect of public speaking?

Other Comments:

15 *Special Occasion Speeches*

Terms to Know

- Speech of Introduction
- Speech of Presentation
- Speech of Acceptance
- After Dinner Speech

We have explored the two primary types of speaking, informative and persuasive, but there are occasions that merit a different type of speech, these are called Special Occasion Speeches. For example, giving a toast a wedding, introducing a keynote speaker at convention, or offering a eulogy at a funeral are all examples of special occasion speeches. While all of these include information they are not traditional informative or persuasive speeches, the unique qualities of these types of presentations will be discussed in this chapter.

Types of Speeches

Speech of Introduction: This speech is designed to draw attention to the main speaker. For example, a key note speaker at a conference, the guest speaker at a business luncheon, the person giving the commencement address at a graduation ceremony these people are typically introduced by another person. This speech is usually brief (less than 3 minutes), but has a few key goals that must be attained. When giving a speech of introduction a speaker has two primary objectives.

The first goal is to build enthusiasm for the speaker. In your presentation you want to get the audience excited for the speaker's presentation. To help craft this you will want to have a biography of the individual. If possible, consult with the person prior to the event to find out if he/she would like you to say something in particular. Make sure you get your information correct; you don't want the main speaker to have to correct your mistakes as part of his or her presentation. Be careful not to praise the speaker too much, if you set the bar too high the speaker can never attain that. For example, think of when a friend says, "I have a joke for you, it's the funniest thing you've ever heard, you'll never hear a joke this funny," is the joke ever *that* funny?

The second goal is to build enthusiasm for the topic. In addition to discussing the speaker you will also want to go over the topic of his or her speech. You want to get the audience excited for the presentation. Apply your audience analysis skills to this task and ask yourself, "Why should the audience want to listen?"

If you are giving a speech of introduction consider using the following structure:

A. Use an attention-getter.	For instance, you might provide a very brief story about the person.
B. Address the audience.	They're still of primary importance, both for you and the other person. Welcome them, and briefly give them an indication that hearing from or at least meeting the other person is valuable.
C. Identify accomplishments.	Here, begin to introduce the speaker in more detail, citing his or her achievements and discussing why they're at this occasion (if that's not already obviously known). Avoid using clichés such as "my next speaker needs no introduction . . ."
D. Introduce the person.	Finally, introduce the other person. Again, avoid using clichés such as "without further ado . . ." Just be straightforward.

Speech of Presentation: Have you ever seen a real or fictional depiction of a city Mayor giving the key to the city to a worthy local hero? The Mayor's speech would be a prime example of a speech of presentation. When giving an award, prize or gift to an individual your speech functions with two goals in mind. First, you want to discuss the nature of the award. When was it created, was it named after someone, what are the criteria for winning or being awarded it, these questions will help you craft a speech that highlights the importance of this award. The second goal is to discuss the recipient's accomplishments. What did the recipient do to earn this award? How did he or she meet the criteria for it? As with the Speech of Introduction, be sure to not over praise the individual. Finally, if handing the recipient an object (trophy, plaque, check, etc.) be sure to hold that item in your left hand and pass it to their left hand while shaking hands.

Speech of Acceptance: In many cases when a person has been presented an award he or she will be expected to make a short speech. If you have seen the annual Academy Awards presentation then you've no doubt observed both good and poor speeches of acceptance. To ensure that your speech is well received there are two goals which should be accomplished.

First you want to thank those that are giving the award. This might include the individual, group, organization or agency that is responsible for the award.

The second goal is to thank those people who helped you attaining in your award. Most all successful individuals have had some help or support and this is an ideal time to thank them for all their support of you.

Two final suggestions are to thank fellow nominees or other finalists if this is a competitive award, and to be brief. A lengthy acceptance speech can foster resentment in your audience.

Speech of Tribute: This speech is designed to give praise for a person or group of individuals. Speeches of tribute could include a wedding toast, speech at a retirement party, a eulogy, or a speech at a birthday party. The key to a successful speech of tribute is to be honest and sincere. The odds are that the person giving a speech of tribute is very well acquainted with the recipient of this speech, but one should always check any uncertain facts. You may also discuss how the individual overcame a hardship or adversity. Stories or anecdotes are often shared to offer insight into this person. Finally, when giving a eulogy try to remain emotionally stable, and respect the person's life achievements rather than concentrating on the person's death.

Speech of Commemoration: This type of speech is most frequently heard on national holidays or other important dates. Often you will hear the U.S. President give a memorial address on historical dates of significance to this country including the attack on Pearl Harbor, Fourth of July or the anniversary of the September 11th, 2001 terrorist attack. When giving a speech of commemoration you should remind the audience of the background of the day or event and draw conclusions about the significance of this event to inspire the audience. Appeal to the audience's pathos, being emotionally charged can lend itself to being dynamic in your presentation. Keep the goal of your speech in mind and be well organized.

After Dinner Speech: An After Dinner Speech, also referred to as a Speech to Entertain is a lighthearted, entertaining speech typically given before, during or after a meal. The history of this speech dates back to 19th century England. It is important to recognize that this is should not be a standup routine but rather a well organized speech. Choose a topic carefully as you ideally want a serious topic that can be exposed with humorous perspective (see chart below). Use your natural speaking style. Consider using multiple types of humor including irony, exaggeration, sarcasm, puns, props, attacking authority, self-deprecation and even your delivery can be a source of humor.

Comparison Chart—Topic: Corporate Sponsorship

Informative speech	Persuasive speech	After Dinner Speech
Discuss the prevalence of corporate sponsorship in sports today.	Discuss the problems associated with corporate sponsorship of collegiate athletics, and present viable solutions to the problem.	Illustrate the wild extent to which some companies will go to secure their product at sporting events, in films, and even in K-12 classrooms.

EXERCISES

1) Pick a significant historical figure and pretend you are going to give a speech of introduction. What would you say about this person, how would your introduce them?

2) In 2003 the CCSN baseball team won the Junior College National Baseball Championship. You have been selected to give them the National Championship trophy. Develop a brief Speech of Presentation to honor their achievement.

3) Write a Eulogy for your best friend. What would you comment on? Which events would you reference?